THE GENTLEMAN'S GUIDE TO MOTORING

Published by AA Publishing, a trading name of AA Media Limited, whose registered office is Fanum House, Basing View, Basingstoke, RG21 4EA; registered number 06112600.

A CIP catalogue record for this book is available from the British Library.

ISBN: 978-0-7495-7275-4 (hardback)
ISBN: 978-0-7495-7339-3 (eBook)

First published in 2012
10 9 8 7 6 5 4 3 2 1

A04826

The views expressed in this book are solely those of the author and do not reflect the views or policies of the AA group.

Cover design by Two Associates
Printed in Spain by Rodesa, Rotativas de Estella SA

theAA.com/shop

THE GENTLEMAN'S
GUIDE TO MOTORING

Vic Darkwood

Vic Darkwood is a writer, painter, slave of the Muse and dabbler in the Bacchanalian arts, whose past projects include co-founding *The Chap* magazine in 1998 and writing several tomes, including *The Chap Manifesto*, *The Chap Almanac: An Esoterick Yearbook for the Decadent Gentleman* and *Around the World in Eighty Martinis*.

CONTENTS

To
Olivia Gerrard
and
Anne Jolly

INTRODUCTION

As you sit, blood quietly on the boil, in a 15-mile tailback on the M25; or wince at the string of expletives thrown at you by a muttonheaded lorry driver as punishment for some minor road indiscretion; or contemplate the frightening geometries of certain roundabouts that exist on the outskirts of Swindon, you may be forgiven for questioning why anyone in their right mind would want to get behind the wheel of a motor car in the first place. Somewhere between the invention of the first modern automobile (Karl Benz's Patent-Motorwagen in 1886) and the present day, the romance of motoring seems to have trickled away, until now we are, at best, ambivalent about its charms.

It is estimated that there are over 750 million passenger cars in the world today, but as their numbers have increased exponentially so the pleasures of motoring seem to have dwindled. We have now reached the point where driving a car is merely a commonplace necessity, a means to an end involving school runs, gridlocked roads, tiring motorway journeys (punctuated by occasional stop-offs at humiliating troughs known as 'services'), and tedious days out transporting barely tolerable in-laws to National Trust properties. In one word, the whole enterprise has become insupportably 'vulgar'. If it weren't for the fact that driving one's own vehicle is never likely to be quite as demeaning as being subjected to the horrors of public transport, then we might all have given up on it long ago.

As with the dinosaur, *Perry Como's Christmas Special* and clackers, the golden age of motoring now seems a long way behind us and our love affair with the internal combustion engine has lapsed into a marriage of convenience – or, more precisely, a marriage where one's spouse has grown a bit sloppy over the years, developed annoying habits, fat deposits or nostril hair, but through force of habit and economic necessity is still reluctantly granted house room.

But we should not be meekly resigned to this status quo. Just because most contemporary car design lacks any aesthetic finesse and the majority of our fellow road users often exhibit behaviour no better than slavering beasts, it doesn't mean that those of an independent frame of mind, with poetry in their soul and vim in their trousers, shouldn't take a stab at reclaiming the whole adventure of motoring as the sanctified mission of the gentleman.

The art of motoring obviously requires a complete overhaul, to be reinvented in a form that captures the original spirit of the motor car. The automobile should no longer be a lowly beast of burden but instead a trusty steed designed to take us on a delightful journey into the sublime. We are talking of nothing less than a radical redrafting of the code of the highway, converting it into a philosophy that ranks style and etiquette on an equal footing with the petty rules and regulations of the road. All is not lost. The flame can be rekindled.

For advice on how this renaissance of motoring might be achieved I have turned to the guidance offered by original guide books from the first 70 years of the motor car and used these as an inspiration and a springboard from which to formulate a new ethos of gentlemanly motoring.

Many readers will doubtless have recourse to their own fleet of vintage Daimlers and employ the services of a skilled chauffeur, but, contrary to popular belief, the realm of urbane roadmanship does not have to be the exclusive preserve of the comfortably jewel-drenched. All that is required is a willingness to lead by example:

> *The first requisite for all motorists is that of coolness, and coupled with this should invariably run a strong undercurrent of gentlemanly behaviour. Luckily the road hog is in a distinct minority in the various classes of motoring, but nevertheless there are still a number of people who are not quite so considerate in their driving principles and manners as one would wish to see them; some from selfishness and some from ignorance.*
>
> *How to Drive a Motorcar*, by the staff of *The Motor*, 1920

Gentlemanly driving is something that can be undertaken by almost every stratum of society and depends as much on a man's attitude and mannerliness as it does on the particular model of car he drives. Whether it be doffing your hat when fellow motorists give way, gaily toot-tooting at your neighbourhood postman as you inadvertently mow down his mail cart for the third time that week, or tipping a gnarled old bumpkin leaning over a gate for some scarcely intelligible directions which he fondly imagines have been useful to you, the gent behind the wheel must take it upon himself to inspire and cajole the benighted throng to act in a more civilised fashion.

In the following pages you'll find a comprehensive guide to gentlemanly driving, from the essentials of delegating the maintenance of your vehicle to the etiquette of the road; from advice on dealing with authority to suggestions for improvements to the current system of road signage; from a handy identifying guide to species of fellow motorist to ways of charming your driving examiner.

In 1936 Richard Alexander Douglas stated in his *Common Sense in Driving Your Car*: 'A man's automobile is one of his most cherished possessions. It is woven inextricably into the fabric of his life.' We must ensure that the fabric our motor car is woven into is made of robust thornproof tweed, silk or even spun gold.

CHAPTER ONE

LEARNING TO DRIVE

RITES OF PASSAGE

Learning to drive is one of the great rites of passage of a gentleman's life, on a par with smoking his first briar, mixing his first dry martini, or getting to grips with his first visit to the opium den or bordello. All are pastimes that may fill the neophyte with a certain amount of nervousness, self-doubt and trepidation, but once mastered will hold him in good stead for the rest of his life.

Unless he happens to be one of those annoyingly robust fellows, prone to back slapping, rugby, laughing too loudly in restaurants and taking absolutely everything in his stride, then getting behind the wheel of a car and switching on the engine for the first time can seem rather daunting. The idea of one and a half tons of cold metal suddenly springing into life and being at one's beck and call like some great huge throbbing anvil of doom... on wheels (**Fig. 1**) naturally needs a certain amount of getting used to and brings with it a heavy weight of responsibility. These days, the law stipulates that before he is allowed to drive solo, the learner driver must demonstrate that he is level-headed, trustworthy and skilled at manoeuvring his vehicle, and as long as he is capable of faking this for the 40 minutes it takes to pass the test, he is then free to join the ranks of the other crazed imbeciles who inhabit our public highways.

ACQUIRING A DRIVING LICENCE

These days the novice gentleman motorist must acquire a provisional licence at a cost of £50 prior to driving his vehicle for the first time and after purchasing it he is only allowed to drive whilst accompanied by a qualified driver. On applying for this licence, he must sign a form confirming that, among other things, he is not prone to 'blackouts', 'periods of confusion' or 'repeated attacks of sudden disabling giddiness'. It is a little tricky for a gent fond of the loucher resorts of Soho to answer such impertinent enquiries entirely honestly, but it is suggested that he responds in the spirit in which the question is put and confirm that, behind the wheel at least, he is prepared to forgo such pleasures.

Such stringent vetting of potential drivers was not always the way of things. In the past any Tom, Dick or Harry could get his hands on a full licence in return for a few morsels of spare change:

> *Every motor driver must be in possession of a driving licence, which has to be taken out before he may have a single lesson on the road. The possession of a licence does not indicate that the holder is a fit and proper person to*

Fig. 1 One's first encounter with a motor car can cause the imagination to stray into strange and disturbing territory.

be in charge of a motor vehicle, though in some countries applicants have to pass examinations before driving licences will be issued. This has long been a topic of discussion among motorists and the non-motoring public, as at present any person whether lame, halt, or blind, can take out a driving licence by obtaining an application form from the County Council or County Borough in which he resides, and the licence will be issued on payment of five shillings.

Richard Twelvetrees, *All About Motoring*, 1924

Sadly the authorities no longer trust the driver to reach an adequate level of proficiency merely at his own whim and, like a trained sea lion, he is required to jump through a series of demeaning hoops before a full licence can be granted.

After years of suggestions and months of discussion driving tests have been made compulsory for all who would obtain a driving licence and who have not held one prior to April 1st 1934.

Humfrey Symons, *How to Pass the Driving Test*, 1935

The test remained voluntary for 14 months between 1st April 1934 and 1st June 1935, when it was finally made compulsory, but unfortunately all the lame, halt, blind, inept and lunatic drivers who had purchased a driving licence prior to 1934 were still legally allowed to drive on the roads. At least some comfort could be gained from the fact that, given another 50 years and a British diet consisting mainly of cigarettes and lard, by the 1980s the roads would be almost free from the dangerously inept motorists of the pre-war generation.

FAMILIARISING YOURSELF WITH THE CONTROLS OF YOUR VEHICLE

Prior to 1934, purchasing a car was similar to buying a new washing machine, DVD player, personal computer or vibrating shiatsu massage chair today. Once it had been ordered and unceremoniously dumped at your doorstep, it was down to you to work out how on earth to get the blighter to function correctly. The only hope a gentleman had was to persuade the salesman to take pity on him and linger a while:

> *Before the expert takes his departure, he should be requested to show exactly what must be done to pilot the car from the road into the garage. The precise spots where the steering wheel must be turned to avoid obstacles, where the brakes ought to be applied; and when all this has been demonstrated he should let the owner take the wheel himself and drive the car in and out several times until he can make the passage unaided, without the risks of damaging the car.*
>
> *The man who has a new car driven into his own garage and then finds it impossible to drive it out owing to lack of skill is about on a par with Robinson Crusoe, who built his boat too far away from the water.*
>
> Richard Twelvetrees, *All About Motoring*, 1924

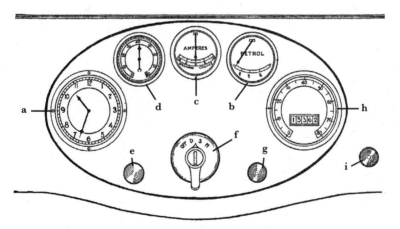

Fig. 2 Elements of the Dashboard as Perceived by the Novice
(**a**) Clock. (**b**) A helpfully-labelled petrol gauge – for gauging your reserve of petrol. (**c**) An amp meter – presumably for gauging your reserve of amperes. (**d**) A spare gauge – in case the other two stop working. (**e**) Possibly a cigar lighter. (**f**) Something to do with the heater? (**g**) A reserve cigar lighter. (**h**) Speedometer – for impressing friends with your blood-curdling velocity. (**i**) Surely, not a third cigar lighter?

These days a gent usually learns how to drive before he purchases his first vehicle. If possible it is desirable to ask a relative or a friend if you can spend some hours sitting in the driving seat of their static vehicle swotting up on the position of all the dials, pedals and levers. **Fig. 2** shows the confusing array of gauges and knobs you might come across in a car of a 1960s vintage and the novice's educated guess at their possible usage. If you find it all hopelessly confusing it is perhaps wise to get a friend to tell you precisely what everything does.

Fig. 3 A resourceful cove utilises his fireplace fender and a poker to construct a frighteningly realistic simulacrum of the driving environment.

I strongly advise the beginner to spend some time in learning the controls before attempting a journey on the road... There is far more chance at becoming proficient quickly if one is content to spend a day in mastering the controls when the car is stationary in the private garage, than by wobbling down the road and making weird and undignified noises with the engine and gearbox.

Richard Twelvetrees, *All About Motoring*, 1924

This is very good advice. Experiment, for example, with changing gears and using the foot pedals. This is best done whilst making appropriately loud accelerating noises and emulating the sound of screeching brakes whilst flinging yourself hectically from left to right, mimicking gangster-like swerves at the steering wheel. In this way, you have a good chance of reaching a certain level of proficiency and developing your own distinctive driving style before hitting the road.

If lack of readies, family or friends means that you simply have no access to a vehicle then it might be a good idea to recreate the driving experience in the comfort of your own home:

If you have neither car nor friend, pull a chair up to the fireplace, put your feet on the fender with the heels on the floor, and hold a short stick in your left hand to represent the gear lever.

Colonel Harold Atherton, *Simplified Motoring*, 1938

Fig. 3 shows how this advice is put into action. In place of the 'short stick' recommended above, this gent uses a more evocative poker to simulate the gear lever. This technique is particularly effective in the long winter months when the gentleman can 'multi-task', learning to drive whilst simultaneously toasting crumpets before the blaze. One note of caution, however: the toasting of crumpets should never be attempted when you are behind the wheel of a real vehicle in motion, even if the road ahead is clear of oncoming traffic and your glowing dashboard cigar lighter makes such a thing seem rather tempting.

ENGAGING THE SERVICES OF
A DRIVING INSTRUCTOR

Instead of trying to muddle through in front of your own hearth, it is probably better to engage the help of an instructor to advise on the niceties of driving technique. As we have already mentioned, if you decide to learn to drive at the controls of an actual moving vehicle you must be accompanied by a licence-holding driver. This might be a friend, a relative or your spouse. Up until fairly recently, of course, a person of this description may well have turned out to be one of the aforementioned 'unqualified' pre-war drivers and would very possibly be utterly clueless as to what knowledge to impart:

> *If you do decide to learn with a friend or relative – and there is a car available for instruction – make sure at the outset that the proposed instructor is an able and experienced driver with a compatible temperament. Unfortunately, many experienced drivers have never passed the test and are unaware of its requirements.*

Michael Austin, *Learning to Drive a Car*, 1961

A 'compatible temperament' is a very important consideration. There is little point in trying to master the intricacies of car control, for example, if you happen to be under the supervision of a wife whose birthday you have managed to forget for the third year running that very morning. It is highly unlikely, in her heightened state of nervous hysteria, that she will turn out to be an encouraging and sympathetic teacher. In fact, such a set-up could be downright dangerous. Approaching a red traffic light, she may suddenly encourage you to speed up, with the words: 'Accelerate! Accelerate, you bastard! My life isn't worth living anyway. I should have listened to my mother...' and so forth, which does not bode well for your prospects of impressing a driving examiner. Likewise, a close chum with whom you share a fondness for gritty debate might be the very ticket when heatedly discussing the relative merits of, say, Picasso versus Braque, whilst in the public bar of the Dog and Duck, but may well turn out to be ruddy useless as a driving instructor. Trying to negotiate the Hanger Lane gyratory system whilst being showered with blows or shaken by the neck in response to your radical views on Nietzsche's concept of eternal recurrence (**Fig. 4**) cannot ever be termed helpful.

It is a far better idea and a great deal safer to engage the services of a trained professional. Driving instructors come in all shapes, sizes and temperaments, but mercifully (unlike friends and family) they are paid to be dispassionate.

This is not to say, however, that driving instructors are without their own psychological quirks. Like war veterans, most instructors will suffer from varying degrees of post-traumatic stress syndrome thanks to the aberrant practices of their students.

Fig. 4 Choose your driving instructor wisely. Being shaken by the neck like a rag doll is not conducive to a safe learning experience.

Most driving instructors have had very nerve-shattering experiences with learners who have jammed a foot hard on the accelerator when they meant to use the brake.

Richard Twelvetrees, *All About Motoring*, 1924

Being contained within a mobile metal box under the perilous control of a string of gawky novices does tend to lend an instructor a certain eccentricity of manner. Even if you are convinced that you are thoroughly competent behind the wheel, your instructor's reactions may say otherwise (**Fig. 5**). He may jump at the slightest noise, cry without reason, or develop a pronounced nervous tic. As in times of war, the constant presence of danger may affect him in other ways too. The proximity of imminent carnage (literally at every turn) and the stricture that he must always conduct himself with utmost propriety, even when teaching a young lady with shapely ankles, may result in a barely contained concupiscence. The author has personally experienced the result of such repression; his own driving instructor

Fig. 5 The learner driver should avoid any outré manoeuvres that may cause distress to his driving instructor.

being prone to leering unattractively through the windscreen at passing ladies on the pavement and muttering under his breath: 'I wouldn't mind feeding bread to *her* ducks.' Naturally, the fellow had to be dismissed after several instances of this. The coarse sentiments of the lower middle classes should not be allowed to pollute a gentleman's sensibilities.

It is of course possible to find an instructor more suited to a gentleman's needs:

> *The study of motoring as an art will afford them much interest in the years that follow. They will think of their driving instructor as gratefully as one thinks of any other who has initiated one into agreeable mysteries.*
>
> Humfrey Symons, *How to Pass the Driving Test*, 1935

By 'agreeable mysteries' we assume that Mr Symons refers to the tobacco, alcohol and bordello scenario mentioned at the beginning of this chapter and, if so, nobody in their right mind could possibly question such sentiments.

PREPARING FOR YOUR DRIVING TEST

Much like taking exams in RE or Geography, the driving test is a colossal waste of time for the gentleman, who has far better things to do than perform party tricks for the Driving Standards Agency, but perform tricks he must. The DSA insists that the trainee driver should master several demeaning pieces of choreography to demonstrate his competence at the wheel and, since 1996, learner drivers are also required to pass a theory test (performed on a damn-fool computer) *prior* to being able to take a stab at the practical exam. There was a time when a gent could stumble into his driving exam directly from a night at Annabel's, have a quick guess at answering the questions in the oral exam and then stumble out again a fully qualified driver largely by the ordinances of chance, but now those days are sadly behind us and a learner really needs to know his onions.

To achieve the required standard the novice must put in quite a number of hours of practice. In the early days of motoring the beginner would ask a friend or relative to drive his new car to a spot where his first faltering attempts at the controls would cause the least inconvenience to other drivers and the least cheek-burning mortification to himself.

> *Make for the most solitary stretch of road you know of. The novice does not require any sort of audience when learning to drive.*
>
> The Autocar magazine, *Useful Hints and Tips for Automobilists*, 1906

The same rule applies today. A capable and compassionate instructor, recognising a gentleman's rarefied soul, will make doubly sure that he is not required to make an utter ass of himself in front of hoi polloi, with the resultant loss of respect for their betters that this might incur. When he has started to get the hang of things and his confidence grows, the gent will of course progress onto busier thoroughfares, but until he finally passes his test (and even after that) he should be wary of the less-than-helpful attitude of fellow motorists:

> *The "L" driver should appreciate there are few so-called experienced drivers prepared to show mercy on the road. Suppose the "L" driver is held at a red light, he is the first in a queue, and he is on the brow of a hill. When the time comes to set off the beginner gets excited or is too eager, with the result that he stalls the engine. Then the trouble begins. A selfish driver gets impatient and sounds his horn, this further excites the learner and he "goes to pieces".*
>
> Lawrence Nathan, *Car Driving in Two Weeks*, 1963

Despite hectoring from the wings, the novice must go through his routine repeatedly until it finally comes as second nature. Some of the parlour games that the DSA insist that he masters will include performing an emergency stop, turning the vehicle to face in the opposite direction using the forward and reverse gears (three-point turn), reversing around a corner and also, from 1991, reverse parking. Unaccountably, the driving test does *not* include swerving, skidding about or narrowly avoiding pedestrians whilst driving at high speed – which are arguably far more difficult feats to pull off with grace and panache.

Your instructor will take you through each stage of these requirements. *Reversing around a corner,* for example, will take place on a quiet back street, where after several mind-numbing lessons involving clutch control, steering locks and blind spots you will no doubt have grasped the prosaic nub and gist of it several times over, and be able to perform the manoeuvre with your eyes shut. But beware: when it comes to the test, keeping your eyes shut may well be held against you, as will any other form of straying from convention. Displaying your creativity through the description of a series of elegant arabesques for example (**Fig. 6b**) might be impressive to friends or those appreciative of the arts, but will be marked down when it comes to taking the actual exam. Unlike judges of ballroom dancing or synchronised swimming, a driving examiner rarely gives extra points for artistic interpretation.

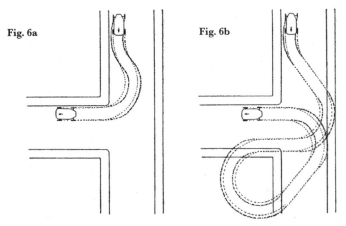

Figs. 6a & 6b When reversing around corners, a prosaic manoeuvre (**a**) is generally deemed preferable by an examiner to the impressive rococo tour de force (**b**).

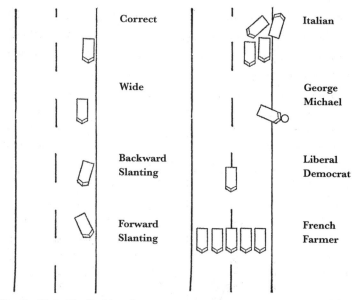

Fig. 7 Kerbside Parking Some commonly observed deviations from the Driving Standards Agency recommended parking technique.

Similar standards of circumspection should be observed when performing parallel parking. A crisp, non-embellished manoeuvre is required, with your vehicle coming to rest in a neat and even proximity to the kerb. **Fig. 7**, adapted from an original illustration in *Car Driving in Two Weeks* by Lawrence Nathan, 1963, shows the various pitfalls and local variations that might be encountered by the unsuspecting gentleman motorist.

TAKING THE TEST

When a gentleman consents to have his abilities put to the test by the designated authorities, he does so under extreme duress. The idea of keeping an appointment for anything other than social reasons is bad enough, but then having to be judged on the basis of a tawdry performance, as if he were Torvill and Dean or some dreadful little dressage pony, is almost too much to bear. As he sits in the reception room of his local test centre, he must try to purge himself of all negative thoughts. At this point he is likely to experience a variety of anxiety symptoms all adding up to a bout of PEST or Pre-Examination Syndromic Trauma. **Fig. 8** shows the tell-tale signs that the gentleman might expect to experience. Normally, such symptoms could be easily cured by the consumption of half a bottle of 15-year-old Ardbeg malt whisky, but this is no normal situation, and quaffing alcoholic beverages before taking one's driving test cannot be recommended. Knocking back several Valium prior to taking the exam is equally foolhardy. Nothing is more likely to raise the hackles of a driving examiner than if you happen to fall sound asleep over the steering wheel halfway through reversing into a side street. No, the distressed gentleman must

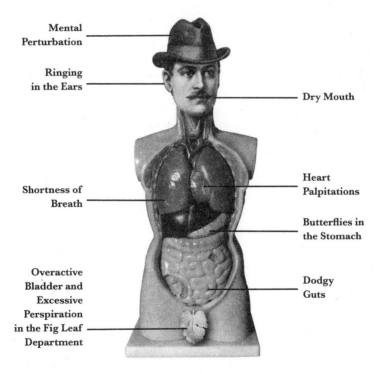

Fig. 8 Illustrating the principal symptoms of PEST (Pre-Examination Syndromic Trauma).

just grin and bear it and content himself with inhaling several deep breaths before taking the plunge.

There is not the slightest need to be afraid of your examiner. As a rule, examiners are quite nice, ordinary people, but they have a responsible job to do, and they have strict instructions as to the way in which they are to do it. Don't be upset if perhaps the examiner appears either coldly official or even positively grumpy. Remember that it is an exacting, boring job, and that he may just have come back in rather a nervous state, after examining an unfit driver who has scared him stiff.

Colonel Harold Atherton, *Simplified Motoring*, 1938

Under the circumstances it is difficult to muster much sympathy for an examiner who holds the power in his hands either to ordain you as a fully fledged member of the motoring fraternity or to condemn you to the degrading hell that is pedestrianism. At this point, it might occur to those of a rash temperament to try to weight things in their favour, conjuring up various ruses by which to influence proceedings. One such tactic is to turn up to the test in full morning dress complete with top hat and in your ancestral 1927 Rolls-

Fig. 9 Driving examiners are rarely perceptive enough to respond to elegance.

Royce Phantom I (**Fig. 9**). This technique involves sauntering over to the examiner and nonchalantly tapping him on the shoulder with one's cane, intoning a phrase such as: "My good man, I do hope this tiresome business won't take long. I have a tea appointment at four with Lady Asquith." The thinking behind this is that the examiner will be so star-struck, not to say intimidated, in the presence of such grandeur that he will simply fail to notice all the appalling mistakes you happen to be making during the course of the test. Sadly, such tactics rarely work. For a start, the sheer length of a Phantom I is likely to make performing a three-point turn a living hell and throw up more problems than it actually cures. Not to mention the fact that a driving examiner is a crack-trained individual, well tutored to be ever vigilant to this sort of jiggery-pokery (and he could well be a damned Socialist to boot).

It is a fact that the examiner gets into the car hoping to pass the candidate, and it is not your face or your manner which will impress him. Only your ability as a driver will pass you; and ladies, he is not looking at your knees, but at your feet! Any offer of a bribe would be reported immediately by the examiner. He will not accept tips, and any attempt to tip him would lead to trouble and embarrassment. It is rewarding enough for the examiner to see your face light up with the smile of success.

Felix Johnson, *How to Pass the Driving Test*, 1964

Yes, the best plan is to meet the fellow with a steady eye and submit to his ludicrous demands without quibble. The first thing an examiner will ask you to do is to read a car registration plate at a distance of 20 metres (or 25 yards). This should be easy enough, but failure to do so will mean that you will instantly fail the test there and then. It is recommended that you practise on parked vehicles before booking your test. **Fig. 10** (overleaf) is a diagnostic chart which demonstrates various disturbances of vision that a gentleman may suffer from and what they may indicate medically.

a. Normal Vision (20/20)

b. Myopia (short-sighted)

c. Esotropia (cross-eyed)

d. Macular Degeneration

e. Paranoid Schizophrenia

Fig. 10 The 20-metre eyesight test – a diagnostic chart for the gentleman hypochondriac. Find out what your eyesight says about your health.

Next, the examiner will ask you to get into your vehicle and set off. Make sure you fasten your seat belt with the exaggerated movements of a children's entertainer and, following this, ensure that you theatrically look in the mirror at regular intervals throughout the test, perhaps in a manner based on something you saw Gielgud do in that marvellous play at the Cottesloe. The mere fact of you using the mirror is not enough for an examiner. One's proficiency must be *demonstrated*. Likewise with every aspect of the test. Be quietly studious and act for all the world as if you haven't even noticed the ruddy-faced civil servant glowering in the seat next to you.

> *Be quietly polite towards your examiner, but don't go out of your way to try to ingratiate him, and don't upset his thoughts with a lot of idle chatter.*
> Colonel Harold Atherton, *Simplified Motoring*, 1938

At some point on your test, the examiner will explain that he will shortly require you to make an emergency stop. The timing of this will be indicated by him hitting the dashboard with his clipboard or a rolled-up newspaper. This is where you really must keep your wits about you, as most gentlemen have a propensity for daydreaming and reverie. By the time you have mirror-signal-manoeuvred back onto the highway and travelled a further couple of hundred yards, it is highly likely that your recent little chat will be nought but a dim and distant memory, and when the examiner finally gets around to thwacking the dash you will not have the foggiest idea what he's up to and probably will blithely assume that he is attempting to swot an annoying bluebottle. Clarity will no doubt dawn only after he testily hits for the third time and a panic-stricken gent is likely to jam his foot on the brake so violently that the entire contents of the back seat (maps, overcoats, cushions, etc) will end up wrapped about the examiner's ears, and once again you will be condemned to the ignoble life of the pedestrian.

Other errors of judgement that might attract the opprobrium of the examiner will include proceeding without due care and attention.

When hovering at the entrance of a side street seeking ingress onto a main road, for example, one must judge when it is sufficiently clear to proceed. Dally a little too long and you might be deemed a ditherer; fling yourself forward on disks of burning rubber and you will be marked down as dangerously reckless. On the whole, if a gent *must* fail the test, he would probably prefer to be damned for his impetuosity.

> *Getting across without a scratch will not satisfy the examiner. He knows that a learner driver has not had sufficient experience to judge safely the speed of oncoming traffic. He is aware of the overall stopping distance required. Therefore, if in doubt, wait. The car whose path you are planning to cut across may be at 80 m.p.h! The driver may be 80 years old, too, and couldn't stop if he wanted to.*
>
> Michael Austin, *Learning to Drive a Car*, 1961

In the end, as long as you keep an eye out for all these eventualities, then everything should be plain sailing. Treat your examiner in the straight manner you might reserve for other busybodies you encounter in life and he should treat you straightforwardly in return.

> *Many stories are in circulation about the driving examiner and the test. "If he asks you for the time, ignore it, he is trying to trap you." This is a favourite. Driving examiners have little time between tests and certainly not the time to be wasted on foolish jokes. There are no tricks or traps in the test. This instance may have occurred because he forgot his watch and had to keep to the time-table.*
>
> Felix Johnson, *How to Pass the Driving Test*, 1964

On returning to the test centre the examiner will reveal his verdict. Expect the same impassive poker face whatever the result. A gent should receive good or bad news with equanimity and on no account be moved to strike or verbally abuse the examiner if he has committed the terrible error of failing you.

CHAPTER TWO

PURCHASING A MOTOR CAR

CHOOSING ONE'S FIRST CAR

A motor car represents one of the largest single outlays of cash that a gentleman will be required to shell for during his lifetime. Its expense will no doubt only be surpassed by such things as the settling of wagers, purchasing a residence (or residences) and paying off his divorce settlement (or settlements).

Unlike selecting which school to send one's offspring to or opting to start a military campaign in the Middle East, choosing the perfect vehicle is not a task that can be undertaken lightly on the spur of the moment and with very little by way of research. No, a gentleman should apply himself to the task with the same solemn deliberation that he might reserve for picking the winner of the Derby, deciding which hat to purchase or alighting upon the perfect combination of cheeses to complement a 1963 bottle of Taylor's Vintage Port (**Fig. 1**).

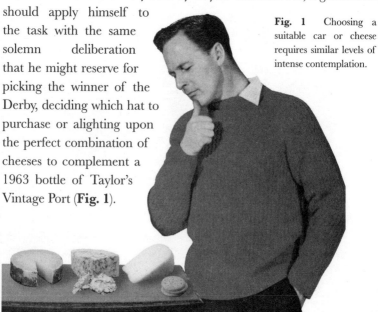

Fig. 1 Choosing a suitable car or cheese requires similar levels of intense contemplation.

Prior to marching down to one's local motor dealer and coughing up the readies, one must embark upon a great deal of cogitation. These days, those searching for information on models of motor car may be inclined to look things up on the 'World Wide Wireless' using their damn-fool personal computers, but a gentleman, suspicious of such modernism, may instead wish to educate himself by seeking the recommendations of friends. But be careful: this may not always be the most advisable course of action:

> *With the best intentions in the world one's motoring friends may prove a regular nuisance in offering advice on buying a new car. The enthusiasm of the private motorist about the make of car he uses is apt to develop into a kind of fanaticism.*
>
> Richard Twelvetrees, *All About Motoring*, 1924

On balance, it is probably sensible to head down to one's local reference library and read all the available literature on the subject, only then making an informed decision based on various essential criteria. These will include your preferences of design, performance and colour; the purpose for which your vehicle will be used; its ability to assuage the wrong-headedness of your spouse; and, more importantly, its ability to satisfy the parsimony of your bank manager.

As a gentleman's *purpose of use* will generally consist of swanning about a bit, dashing around like a maniac or simply showing off, we need not cover this in any great depth here. Similarly with performance, this can immediately be ascertained by levelling an appropriately phrased question to the car salesman, such as: 'Does she go some?' or 'She'll knock spots off the competition, what?' This enquiry should be accompanied by a hearty slap on the back of the salesman, along with a broad manly wink. An answer in the affirmative will tell the gentleman all he needs to know, or indeed all he is likely to understand, regarding CCs, litres, fuel efficiency, cylinders, horsepower and the like.

COST

Unless he is blessed with the sort of income that might be generated by a portfolio of estates covering five-eighths of the West Country, the aspirant gentleman car owner will probably need to kowtow to a budget. As with his encounters at the gaming table, the cocktail cabinet or the pudding trolley, he will most likely set himself a strict limit and then immediately capitulate the moment he is confronted with anything approximating temptation. Nevertheless, for appearance's sake he will make it his mission to at least give an impression of sober reflection. If all else fails, taking his wife along to the car showroom or making a quick phone call to his bank manager is likely to put him back on the straight and narrow far more efficiently than any attempts at self-control.

No matter what a gentleman's circumstances he will no doubt find some way of conjuring up the requisite spondulicks to join the ranks of the motoring classes, even if he has to resort to arrangements of a frankly vulgar nature:

> *In years gone by it was regarded as very dreadful to purchase anything by deferred payments, for genteel people who wanted things without having enough money to pay for them much preferred to accept long credit without entering into 'stupid agreements'. Fortunately, perhaps, a wide recognition of the method of deferred payments has opened up the possibility of motoring for many who could not afford to buy cars outright, and every year more and more cars are being sold by this very convenient method.*
>
> Richard Twelvetrees, *All About Motoring*, 1924

If the impecunious gentleman motorist can put up with the ostracism from polite society that deferred payments entail, then they do at least have the advantage of setting back the final payment on his vehicle for several generations to come, allowing him to live like a crazed adolescent for today and leave it to his great-grandchildren to pick up the final tab.

DESIGN AND SIZE

Experts agree that the death of car design occurred somewhere between the last Triumph Vitesse rolling off the production line in 1971 and the publication of J.G. Ballard's *Crash* in 1973. After this (with the possible exception of one or two models produced by the Morgan Motor Company), all cars began to resemble tedious household items such as food mixers, hi-fi systems, plastic egg cartons or Hoovers, and as absolutely nothing could induce a gentleman of quality to suffer the indignity of travelling in a domestic appliance, henceforth he would elect to drive almost exclusively in vehicles of vintage origin.

There is an essential checklist that the motoring gent needs to tick off when selecting a vehicle. This will include questions such as:

1) Does it feature lashings of chrome, nickel silver or brass?

2) Does the bodywork include preposterously flamboyant wings?

3) Does the design ethos of the vehicle pay scant attention to considerations of practicality?

4) Will it tend to make one's friends and associates positively emerald with envy?

5) Will ordinary members of the public look frightened or gawp in slack-jawed wonderment at its approach?

If the answer to at least two of these questions is *yes*, then it would seem that the gentleman driver is at least proceeding in the correct spirit.

Next he must apply his discerning eye to the car's interior. This should contain the sort of features guaranteed to give a gentleman a comfortable and sedate ride. In the front seat, the dashboard should be set out ergonomically, with all essential features such as steering wheel, Bakelite wireless, pipe rack, snuff tray and cigar lighter within comfortable reach (**Fig. 2**, overleaf). As far as the rear seat of a car's interior is concerned, the potential purchaser should make sure that it is at least equipped with a combination involving some of the following: veneered woodwork, chrome ashtrays, leather armrests, antimacassars and a fully stocked mirror-lined cocktail cabinet with enough gin, vermouth and olives to see both driver and passenger through the trauma of at least three chilly nights stranded in the middle of nowhere.

Other than this, there may be some practical considerations to take into account:

Remember that when you go motoring, whether on business or pleasure, you are perfectly certain to take 'things' with you, such as luggage, or luncheon baskets or parcels. Choose if you can, a car whose body work is upholstered in real leather, and not in any substitute.

John Prioleau, *Motoring for Women*, 1925

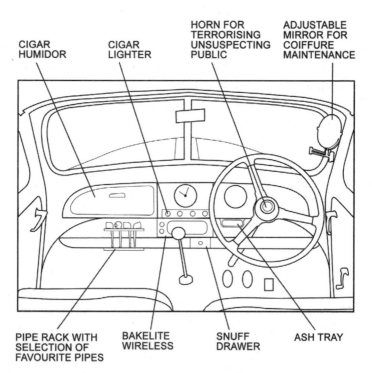

Fig. 2 The ideal arrangement of the features essential for the maximum convenience of the driver, thus ensuring a comfortable driving experience.

Mr Prioleau is completely correct in his assertion that leather is the preferred upholstery option, but the gentleman does not like to have his interior design dictated by the requirements of mundane freight, such as packages, suitcases or corpulent maiden aunts. Although, with one's maiden aunt's corpulence in mind, perhaps the following advice might come in useful:

> *You can generally take it for granted that however large a car you buy (large, I mean, in seating capacity) you will never find it too large.*
>
> John Prioleau, *Motoring for Women*, 1925

The size of a car is indeed frightfully important, not only for practical considerations such as accommodating a particularly large brood of offspring, ease of parking or negotiating tight corners, but also for how it complements the bearing of the driver. To help gauge this see **Fig. 3**, taken from Charles Baudry de Saunier's *The Art of Motor Driving* (1909), where precise measurements are given regarding arm and leg room.

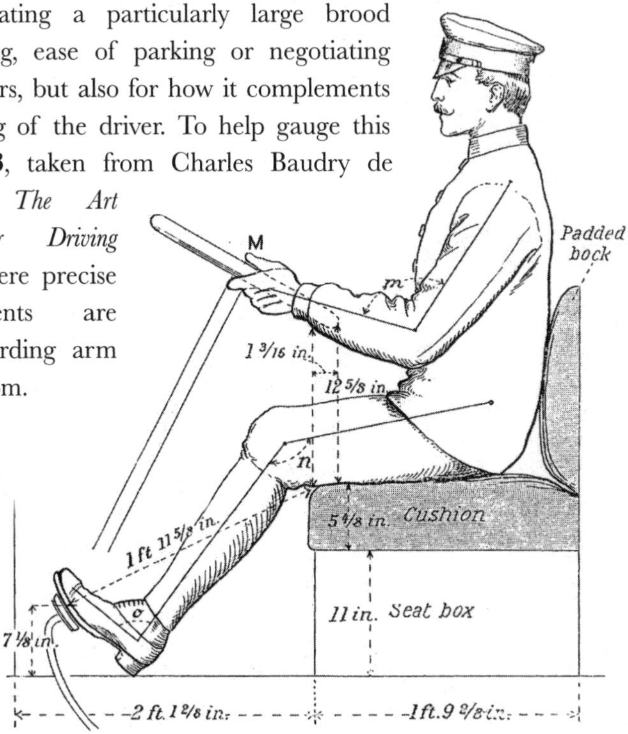

Fig. 3

A driver should also ensure that his chosen vehicle 'suits' him stylistically. If he chooses wrongly then he may become a figure of ridicule or, even worse, pity. Like a beautifully tailored suit, a car should be a perfect fit, enhance a gentleman's physique and serve to iron out any of his physical imperfections. A particularly short man, for example, should opt for a modest-sized vehicle, with extra padding on the driving seat to facilitate seeing out of the window. Likewise, a very large man should opt for a far more spacious vehicle as he is bound to look idiotic if he attempts to spoon his blubbery bulk into the driving seat of a miniscule motor car such as the Mini.

THE PSYCHOLOGY OF CAR COLOUR

When we select the colour of our car we are inadvertently broadcasting subliminal messages to all around us as to our confidence, vulnerability or general state of mind. Some research has been brought to the author's attention which analyses the important psychological effect that colour can have on car drivers. According to a study carried out in 1994 by psychologist Conrad King, owners of pastel-coloured cars are eight times more likely to suffer from depression than people with brightly coloured cars, whereas drivers of white cars tend to be a bit stand-offish and owners of silver or metallic blue cars turn out to be the most sickeningly content drivers on the road. Unsurprisingly, the veritable marauding alpha apes of the tarmac are those who choose to drive black or red cars.

It is probably better if the gentleman maintains a healthy scepticism regarding such research. Pastel vehicles will obviously tend to be favoured by the ineffectual, the soppy or the natural-born victim, which is as good a reason as any for feeling a bit down in the dumps. The initial bright-eyed enthusiasm of such an owner will suddenly evaporate the instant they become aware of the extra maintenance involved in the ownership of a pastel-coloured vehicle:

> *When a new car is examined in the showroom, all resplendent in its smart appearance, the individual may think how much better it would look if it were finished off in purple, light blue, or some other bright colour. Ladies, of course, are very keen to have smartly finished cars, but one is apt to forget that the ravages of mud and dust will soon destroy the glory of a smart new car.*
>
> Richard Twelvetrees, *All About Motoring*, 1924

Similarly, red or black cars are bound to be looked upon favourably by the ruthless and ambitious, not because such colours are innately empowering, but because such drivers are very likely to be the dull and unimaginative individuals one finds working in the financial sector, for whom *being in the red* or *being in the black* are the two concepts they are capable of getting their limited heads around.

So, while the gentleman driver may allow himself a cheery sneer if he happens to pass a car liveried in Mango Carnival, Peach Sunset or Cerise Blush, he will not place too much emphasis on the colour of a vehicle and concentrate on more important observations, such as its vintage, its exuberant styling and the fiercely creative manner in which it is being handled.

DEALING WITH CAR SALESMEN

Once the gent has a fixed idea as to which style, make and hue of car he is going to buy, then it is time to venture down to a reputable vintage car dealership. Once there, unless he is very careful, within a matter of moments he will have had his resolve completely undermined and, malleable as a Curly Wurly that has been left on top of a hot radiator, he will find himself twisted into any shape that may take the salesman's fancy. As with dining with baboons, swimming with piranhas or bending for the soap in a prison shower, it is imperative to keep your wits about you at all times and not to get too carried away by the first resplendent shiny vehicle that catches your eye:

Fig. 4 The Honest John

It is next to impossible to resist, getting into a beautiful coupé or saloon, or into an artistically finished open car, lying back on the magnificent cushions and imagining yourself to be in the possession of such a super car. At this point a skilled salesman has an excellent chance of getting your order for a car which, in your saner moments, you would not dream of buying.

John Prioleau,
Motoring for Women, 1925

Even if you are dealing with a used-car salesman who dignifies his calling with the epithets *classic* or *vintage*, it is still recommended that you proceed with the greatest trepidation, as all salesmen are essentially animals of prey. Consider consulting an expert independent adviser.

> *Buying a second-hand car is to an enthusiast an entertaining and an instructive proceeding, but it is full of pitfalls, and I would not advise any newcomer to motoring to undertake it except under the expert guidance of an experienced owner-driver.*
>
> John Prioleau, *Motoring for Women,* 1925

In fact, salesmen of any type will try every sickening trick in the book to separate a gent from his hard-inherited cash, so it might be useful here if we outline the various sorts he is likely to encounter. Salesmen may come in all shapes and sizes, but in the final analysis they can be identified as four basic models. The first category is the 'Honest John' (**Fig. 4**), whose salt-of-the-earth burblings should immediately alert the potential buyer to be on his guard. He will tell you he is selling at a loss, that the car has had only one previous owner or that the proceeds of the sale will pay for his dear old mother's eye operation – in fact he is genetically programmed to say *anything* to achieve a sale. There is an outside possibility that you will get a good deal from such a man, but it is far more likely that you'll find yourself comprehensively fleeced.

Secondly, there is the breed of 'respectable' salesmen from an established 'classic' retailer. These will be unattractively unctuous individuals, interchangeable with salesmen everywhere from art galleries to estate agents, sometimes operating in pairs (**Fig. 5**), who will try to win over a customer with a soothing balm of purred insincerity. You will not get a bargain from such sorts but you are at least half-likely to leave with a vehicle that won't fall apart like a clown's car a hundred yards after leaving the car salesroom.

Fig. 5 The Unctuous Duo

Next, we have 'The Enthusiast' (**Fig. 6**), probably ex-RAF, who has set up his own independent classic car company in a dignified town such as Royal Leamington Spa. This man will know his potatoes and may be persuaded to give a substantial reduction on a car as long as he feels as if 'one of his fillies' is going to the right home. However, this will entail several excruciating hours of buttering the fellow up by listening to his interminable motoring anecdotes and quite possibly feigning a service record, an old school tie and a few choice reminiscences of your own.

Fig. 6 The Enthusiast

Finally, if your car salesman looks anything like this (**Fig. 7**), then he is probably best avoided, as unnecessary extravagances in a salesman's dress sense may indicate that he is untrustworthy and even possibly a little bit foreign. This does not bode well for the roadworthiness of any vehicle you might purchase from him.

To avoid the very worst excesses of a car salesman's dark arts and at least reassure yourself that a vehicle you are interested in is: a) capable of starting; b) capable of moving; and c) doesn't spontaneously stop again after ten minutes' use, it is advisable to request a test run. Usually a car dealer will

Fig. 7 The Shady Character

suggest that he accompanies you on such a jaunt, but do all you can to dissuade him, as then you will be able to relax and really put the car through its paces without any consequent tutting, gulping or petrified yelps from the passenger seat. Offer to leave your bank details, your current vehicle (if you have one) or, if all else fails, your children or a copy of your hair-raising diaries. The latter can be quite effective if, as you hand it over, you explain in hushed conspiratorial tones: 'There is enough scandal in there to blow the top off the House of Lords and keep the tabloids busy for a month. Keep it closed and safe, my friend, until I am returned.'

Free from prying eyes, you should now take the vehicle through your various normal routines such as skidding to a halt at a heavily populated zebra crossing, taking your habitual short cut through the municipal flower beds en route to Ye Olde Cheshire Cheese, accelerating over cattle grids, tailgating cyclists up steep inclines and toot-tooting pretty young ladies just to gauge what sort of admiring glances you can muster. If all seems in order, make some derisory offer on your return and allow yourself to be haggled back up to no more than 70 per cent of the asking price.

TEN IDEAL MOTOR VEHICLES FOR THE INDEPENDENTLY MINDED GENTLEMAN

1903 Panhard & Levassor

The ideal car for undertaking the London to Brighton Veteran Car Run. This vehicle allows the driver to indulge in his penchant for dressing up in an interesting array of protective motoring outfits (see Chapter Three) and appeals to a gent's eye through its extensive use of brass fittings.

1919 A.V. Monocar

The far more sleek, stylish, efficient and beautiful precursor of the Sinclair C5, this British cyclecar was manufactured by Ward and Avey of Teddington. The bodywork is charmingly fashioned out of wood, plywood or even compressed paper. Its sleek width of a mere 30 inches and lightweight construction mean that it cannot be recommended for use by those suffering from 'big bones' or suet addiction.

1926 Bugatti Type 35C

The gentleman's dream car – a reminder of the days when the racing rake would set off from home in his Bugatti, drive to the racetrack, down six *pinkers* (Plymouth gin and a dash of Angostura bitters), then compete in the Grand Prix in the car in which he had driven to the track. After the race he might drink some bottles of champagne and some brandy, ravish a couple of serving wenches and still be home in time for tea. When men were men and cars were made of metal.

Circa 1929 Burney Streamline

A revolutionary car created by airship designer Sir Charles Dennistoun Burney, the Streamline, at just under 20 feet long, is not for those cursed with modest driveways or the gent who wishes to park in town centres at peak hours. Featuring a seven-seat interior with headroom designed specifically for hats to be worn, and a cocktail cabinet contained within one of the rear doors, this is the ideal vehicle for the gent who wishes to travel in extreme comfort. Only 12 Streamlines were ever made.

1933 Dymaxion

This three-wheeler was designed by US inventor and architect Buckminster Fuller as part of his grand Dymaxion scheme involving architecture and other design projects. This car may not immediately strike one as a vehicle befitting a gentleman, resembling as it does the progeny of a Volkswagen Camper and a killer whale, but the idealistic intellectual provenance of the vehicle appeals to a gent's rarefied sensibilities. Another 20-footer, only three prototypes were made, although lately the architect Sir Norman Foster has recreated the vehicle.

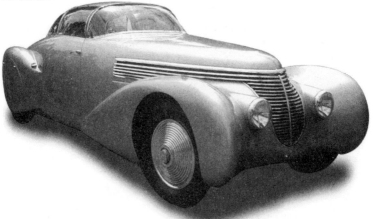

1938 Hispano-Suiza H6C Saoutchik Xenia Coupé

Along with the young Jean Shrimpton, the H6C Xenia is one of the most beautiful sights ever to have registered on the retina of mankind. Unsurprisingly mentioned in P.G. Wodehouse's *Blandings Castle*, it is a car that epitomises the golden age of motoring and its streamlined body, designed by Jacques Saoutchik, shares many features with an aircraft fuselage. The interior is modelled on the cockpit of a fighter plane. Affords an odd combination of reliving the Battle of Britain whilst simultaneously sitting in an Art Deco cocktail lounge.

1947 Bentley Mark VI Franay Drophead Coupé

The gent with a penchant for chrome and wings the size of a Hokusai tsunami need look no further than this 1947 Bentley with custom bodywork by Franay, coachbuilders of Paris. Other features include an interior clad entirely in frog skin and a built-in bespoke bar cabinet complete with glasses and silver flasks. First displayed at the 1947 Paris Auto Show, it is perhaps as good an example as any of the true meaning of *entente cordiale*.

Circa 1952 Jowett Jupiter Convertible

A British car made in Idle near Bradford, the Jupiter, despite being fitted with a bench seat for three people, is ideal for the amorous chap wishing to win the heart of a young lady. Deceptively cuddly but with a savage heart, the gentleman may well find that it closely resembles his own personality, and hopefully its success at Le Mans in 1950 and the Monte Carlo and Lisbon International Rallies in 1951 will be a harbinger of a similar level of achievement in the realm of the bedchamber.

Circa 1958 Alvis TD21 Drophead Coupé

After the stylistic excesses of the previous page, perhaps the more subtle gent will be relieved to be presented with a car that is the epitome of suave understatement. With coachwork by Park Ward, elegant streamlining and optional wire-spoked wheels, the Alvis TD21 seems as comfortable in its own skin as a salami at a chipolata convention. If Beau Brummel had lived in the age of motoring then perhaps this is the car he would have elected to own (and then promptly lost at the gaming tables at White's).

1969 Ponthieu 'Pussycar' Automodule

Some may consider this another unlikely choice for the genteel motorist, but even though this one-off concept car (designed by Frenchman Jean-Pierre Ponthieu) may seem off-puttingly futuristic, it is in fact ideally suited to a gentleman's needs. Powered by a two-stroke 250cc engine, it can't be said to be the fastest-moving vehicle in the world but it does afford ample opportunity for the dandy to flaunt his new wardrobe to an admiring public without going through the gruelling ordeal of actually having to rub shoulders with them.

CHAPTER THREE

WHAT TO WEAR

CUTTING A DASH

Once you have mastered the various controls and abstruse mechanical widgets associated with driving a car, and then purchased a vehicle that you aren't ashamed to be seen dead in (always a sensible precaution), it is time to pose possibly one of the most crucial questions that the fledgling gentleman motorist is ever likely to have to ask himself: 'What in heaven's name is one supposed to wear?'

As luck would have it, vintage motoring manuals and magazines don't stint on advice in this area. Gentleman (and lady) drivers will find themselves positively spoilt for choice by the array of costumes on offer. The style of your outfit will very much depend on the vintage of your car,

Fig. 1 Motoring allows the gent to give vent to some of his more outré tastes in suit design.

the climatic region you are proposing to visit, the relative dimensions of your wallet and the particular dash you are planning to cut. As a default, the gentleman should opt for a three-piece suit constructed out of a sturdy thornproof tweed reinforced externally at the elbows and knees, and, internally in the gusset region, with a fine chamois leather. This latter precaution is designed to reduce unwarranted stress on the testicles and alleviate consequent damage to the seminal vesicles whilst driving over uneven road surfaces or the cobbled streets of former mill towns when on motoring holidays in 't' North'. Excessive jiggling of the nether regions has been scientifically proven to be one of the commonest causes of male infertility.

Those who consider themselves a bit more sporty or flamboyant, and plan to zip about country lanes accompanied by excitable young ladies (with braying laughs that come fitted as standard) can push the sartorial envelope a little by adopting jackets of a loud check or striped material (**Fig. 1**). It is a strange phenomenon that the clothes that would generally be regarded as infra dig in everyday life can become almost acceptable when seen on the golf course or in a speeding 1950 Jowett Jupiter. But be careful, for as early as 1904 Alexander Filson Young warned against excesses in the area of costume:

The kind of clothes one wears when motoring is important. It is evidently thought by some motorists (with a propriety of which they are quite unconscious) that it is necessary to dress themselves in hideous garments.
A.B. Filson Young, *The Complete Motorist*, 1904

Naturally, if this type of motorist were ever to sell his car and return to pedestrian Civvy Street, these motoring togs should be burnt, hidden under the floorboards or given away to a clown in a passing circus.

If you are fortunate enough to be the owner of a car of early construction, say a 1902 Napier Racing Two-Seater (**Fig. 2**, overleaf), a car so manly that the inclusion of such fripperies as a roof, windscreen and doors was considered, frankly, a bit namby-pamby, you are likely to need clothing of far more serious construction. Whatever period of car a gentleman chooses to drive, the following sections will tell you all you are likely to need, or indeed ever want, to know about selecting clothes for all vehicles and all weather conditions.

Fig. 2 The Napier Racing Two-Seater. Possibly the most manly of all cars.

HEADWEAR

Perusing the advertisement pages of early motoring magazines it is possible to compile a full catalogue of useful garments for gents or ladies who are planning to expose themselves to the elements whilst careering along the open highway.

The female motorist is placed in a bit of a quandary in her choice between utility and style. A lady who has preserved and nurtured her complexion carefully over the years through the use of parasols, sun block and moisturising unguents cannot then be expected to cheerfully assent to having her glowing flesh serrated by the action of savage air currents. A full chamois-leather face mask (**Fig. 3**) is the only practical solution to this problem.

As far as hats are concerned, female instinct will usually err on the side of stylistic excess and she will naturally be drawn to ill-proportioned headgear dripping with bows, taffeta, nosegays and agglomerations of fruit, but heed the sage advice of precedent:

It is a pity that women have not yet made up their minds as to the best form of headdress to wear when motoring. The Park presents a sad spectacle on a windy day when many women wear a large hat, and has to keep her hand on it to make it remain on her head. There is a large fortune to be made by any milliner or hatter who can invent a small tight-fitting hat which will stick to it like a grim death.

Lady Jeune, *Autocar* magazine, 1902

The gent, on the other hand, should don a cap of a peculiarly jaunty nature. Whilst a top hat, a trilby or a bowler is perfectly acceptable on occasion, a cap has more of a chance of staying in contact with the cranium at high speeds. A peaked cap of a slightly nautical character might be an option (**Fig. 4**), but it does carry with it the danger of misidentifying one as a chauffeur and nothing is quite so deflating to the spirits as attending a social event only to be mistaken for 'staff',

Fig. 3

MASKS.

This mask cannot be said to be becoming, but it is used largely in Paris by ladies who wish to preserve their complexion.

Fig. 4

GOGGLES.

In large variety, over twenty different designs, with prices ranging from **1/-** to **12/6**

645. " THE BEXHILL " (as illustration), **12/6**

tossed a shilling and handed a bucket and shammy. A better option is a good baggy golfing or cricketing cap. This should preferably be worn at a rakish angle when travelling at speeds over 30 miles per hour to symbolise complete nonchalance in the face of danger.

As we have already established, the manufacturers of early 20th-century models of motor car rather frowned upon extravagant notions such as windows, the driver and his passengers being obliged to make

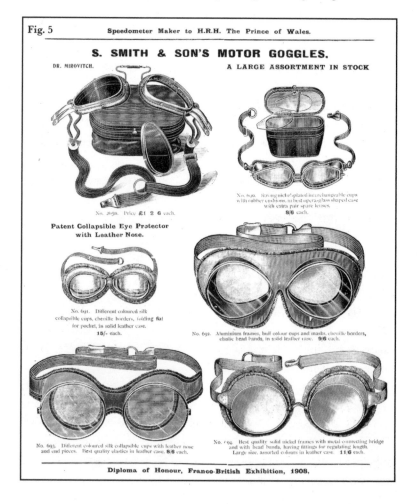

Fig. 5   Speedometer Maker to H.R.H. The Prince of Wales.

S. SMITH & SON'S MOTOR GOGGLES.

DR. MIROVITCH.   A LARGE ASSORTMENT IN STOCK

No. 2050. Price £1 2 6 each.

No. 690. Strong nickel-plated interchangeable cups with rubber cushions, in best opera-glass shaped case with extra pair spare lenses. 8/6 each.

Patent Collapsible Eye Protector with Leather Nose.

No. 691. Different coloured silk collapsible cups, chenille borders, folding flat for pocket, in solid leather case. 18/- each.

No. 692. Aluminium frames, buff colour cups and masks, chenille borders, elastic head bands, in solid leather case. 9/6 each.

No. 693. Different coloured silk collapsible cups with leather nose and end pieces. Best quality elastics in leather case. 8/6 each.

No. 694. Best quality solid nickel frames with metal connecting bridge and with head bands, having fittings for regulating length. Large size, assorted colours in leather case. 11/6 each.

Diploma of Honour, Franco-British Exhibition, 1908.

up for this design oversight by providing their own. A motorist's window onto the road ahead is provided by the use of motoring goggles (**Figs. 4 & 5**).

> *It is... absolutely indispensable that the eyes of the automobilist should be protected from dust, small stones, flies, the painful and even dangerous impacts of big insects like cockchafers, and even from the harmful effects of the air beating upon the eyes at high speeds. The use of goggles, or what is better a windscreen, is necessary for security on driving and for the preservation of the eyes.*
>
> Charles Baudry de Saunier, *The Art of Motor Driving*, 1909

> *For ordinary wear the goggles made of thin convex glass surrounded by an edge of thin silk are quite sufficient; but for very fast travelling the heavier glasses in a ventilated metal framework and with a light leather mask attached are safer and better.*
>
> A.B. Filson Young, *The Complete Motorist*, 1904

Even when driving later models of car, where the use of goggles is not strictly necessary, they can be worn for both stylistic and medical reasons. A large pair of vintage flying goggles (see 'Driver Spotter' on page 80) undeniably imbues a man with a god-like supremacy on the road, leaving fellow motorists, who might wish to argue the toss, in no doubt as to exactly which side their asphalt is buttered. Equally, eye protection can prevent a motorist's ocular orbs from bruising due to excessive rattling in their sockets on repeated encounters with speed bumps in urban areas.

Another absolutely splendid, not to say essential, innovation which blurs the line between personal accoutrement and motoring accessory is a product invented by Alfred Dunhill. One of the first gents ever to have been prosecuted for speeding (in 1903, at a heady 25 miles per hour), and therefore well worth our admiration, Mr Dunhill was so incensed by the injustice of it all that he took it upon himself

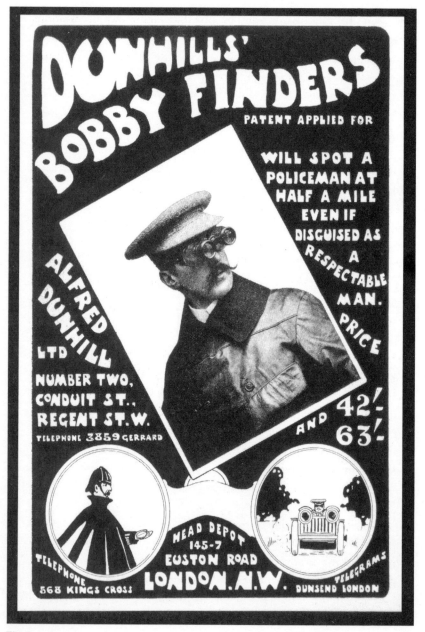

Fig. 6

to abet the motorist in bamboozling the authorities by inventing Dunhill's Bobby Finders (**Fig. 6**). These are essentially a pair of motoring goggles with binoculars fitted to them, but hinged so that they may be brought into and out of action in a trice. Their claim that they could 'spot a policeman at half a mile even if disguised as a respectable man' can only endear us to Mr Dunhill even further and thank him posthumously for his services to gentlemanly motoring.

As if Bobby Finders weren't enough to secure his position as one of the great benefactors of mankind, Mr Dunhill went on to pioneer another accoutrement tailor-made for the gentleman motorist. The Windshield Pipe (**Fig. 7**) is an implement specifically designed to counteract any problems the gent may encounter keeping his briar alight whilst charging tempestuously along the highway. A raised 'windshield' at the prow of the pipe ensures a smooth smoke no matter the speed at which one is travelling.

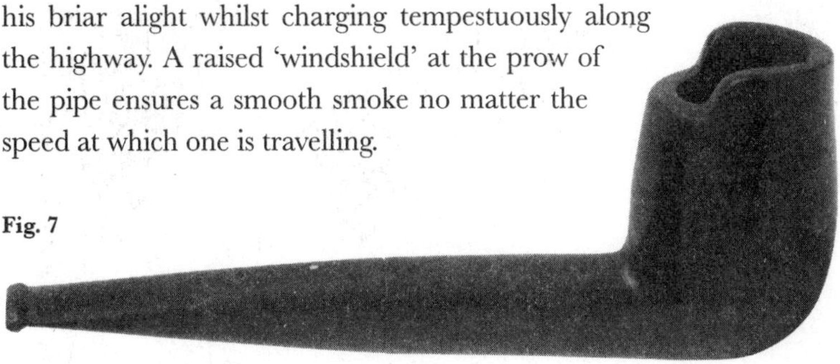

Fig. 7

A further piece of kit that is absolutely essential for the more hirsute gentleman is the moustache snood (**Fig. 8**). These days, despite globalisation and boasts of trans-global shopping convenience

Fig. 8 The Stern moustache snood – the only sensible way of protecting one's sub-nasal shrubbery from the potentially ruinous effects of G-force.

Figs. 9a & 9b Demonstrating the terrible harm that can be inflicted on a gentleman's facial hair by leaving it unprotected from the devastating effects of savage wind currents.

by the so-called World Wide Wireless, items of tash protection are rather difficult to come by, but thankfully there are still manufacturers in existence who cater to the motorist's needs in this department. There is little point in a gent spending several hours in the morning carefully sculpting his handlebar moustache into an object of sublime beauty if his efforts are literally thrown to the wind when he goes a-motoring in the afternoon. The mustachioed fellow who elects to travel by open-top car must therefore take adequate precautions lest his pride and joy reverts from its pristine state (**Fig. 9a**) into a tangled mess at which even the most casually inclined of cavemen would blush (**Fig. 9b**).

OVERCOATS AND DRIVING GLOVES

With the welfare of his head adequately catered for, attention should now be paid to a gent's equatorial regions. He will no doubt have already ordered a pleasing wardrobe of driving suits from a reputable expeditionary tailor such as Norton & Sons of Savile Row, but will need to complement these with a range of over-clothing designed for every vicissitude of climate. Few pleasures are comparable to deliberating over the cut and design of a motoring overcoat (paying due attention to the number and dimensions of pockets so that they may accommodate map, hip flask, sextant, items of road kill and so on) and sharing some witty repartee with your tailor.

For temperate climes, a simple greatcoat with button-over chest shield should be worn (**Fig. 10**), or for the ladies an equivalent cape (**Fig. 11**), but in colder conditions more heavy-duty items need to be adopted. The reindeer coat (**Fig. 12**, overleaf) is very good news for the motorist (though not such good news for the reindeer), the idea being that a pelt designed by nature for withstanding arctic conditions

Fig. 10   **Fig. 11**

Fig. 12

Fig. 13

is bound to make an ideal cold-repelling garment for the chilly gent. By this logic, the advent of polar bear trousers and the whale blubber mackintosh cannot be far off. In the meantime, the best way of dealing with torrential downpours, monsoons and spontaneous deluges is to wear an 'umbrella coat' (**Fig. 13**). Its original manufacturers in 1902 described it thus: 'the neck consists of pure rubber so that there is no button on the garment, and the head is pushed through the elastic orifice provided by the rubber insertion'. If we can ignore a description that sounds like a daunting and thoroughly unpleasant medical procedure then the utility of the item will be found to be invaluable.

Hurtling like a comet along the highway is always calculated to cause a bit of a draught and evasive tactics must be taken to prevent gale-force winds and turbulence from billowing along the sleeves, up the trouser legs and into other apertures. So-called 'storm cuffs' (**Fig. 14**) may be used for this purpose or otherwise the following solution:

It is desirable to sew satinette protectors inside the sleeves and close them with elastic... [which] prevents air and dust from blowing up the sleeve.
Charles Baudry de Saunier, *The Art of Motor Driving*, 1909

A more stylish approach to hand and wrist protection, however, is the gauntlet glove (**Fig. 15**):

As an additional precaution the driver may wear a gauntlet glove which comes up over the cuff... When driving the glove should always be worn, not only for the sake of appearances but also for the cleanliness of the hands.
Charles Baudry de Saunier, *The Art of Motor Driving*, 1909

With its connotations of knights and chivalry, the gauntlet can act on a man's psychology in much the same way as a substantial return on a turf investment or a chance encounter with a rouged showgirl on an expansive night out with the chaps. They are likely

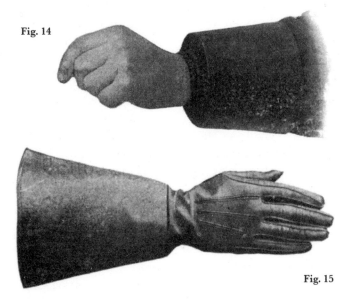

Fig. 14

Fig. 15

to drive up his adrenalin and his blood pressure and care should be taken whilst wearing them not to become swollen with hubris and regard other motorists as no more than mere ants to be crushed beneath one's wheels. Otherwise, they come highly recommended.

Fig. 16

If a gauntlet glove has a tendency to unleash parts of your personality that you'd rather not know about then perhaps you ought to opt for a lighter variety of glove. The string-backed sporting glove (**Fig. 16**) is best suited to later models of car such as the Triumph Vitesse or a 1960s MG and lends a man an air of devil-may-care jauntiness.

TROUSERS, RUGS AND APRONS

It has no doubt been noted by the reader that most of the tenets of a gentleman motorist's dress code are roundly ignored by the bulk of modern-day drivers. Often the average motorist not only neglects to wear a suit but at times may also be observed in various pitiful states of undress involving 'T-shirts', 'denim', vests and, heaven forfend, sometimes no shirt at all. It is perhaps to be regarded as a small mercy that, except in very rare cases attributable to madness, perversity or inebriation, most gents still find it helpful and necessary to wear trousers whilst driving.

Below the waist the gentleman driver is once again presented with an array of options:

The bottom of the trousers should be narrow because, if too large, they are more liable to be soiled and catch on any projections... Some drivers wear knickers, but these are only suitable for touring. Sometimes the knickers are worn in conjunction with garters or puttees and this is a fashion which can be recommended.

Charles Baudry de Saunier, *The Art of Motor Driving*, 1909

A pair of tweed 'knickers' or plus fours is indisputably a very fetching garment and, worn in conjunction with spats as seen in **Fig. 17**, they are almost impossible to surpass as legwear. A variant on this are the intrinsically dapper riding breeches (**Fig. 18**), which regrettably are only really suited to a Mercedes-Benz 770 Nazi staff car. This get-up might be deemed unnecessarily provocative and ostentatious when worn on family shopping expeditions to Asda. Far better to stick with the plus fours, on top of which in inclement weather the driver should use a driving rug:

Fig. 17

Fig. 18

Fig. 19

Waterproof
Foot Muff Apron

(Provisionally protected).

Lined real lambswool, with
pockets for feet. Exceedingly
comfortable, keeping the feet and
ankles thoroughly warm.

In Leather Cloth ... ... **60**'-
In Solid Leather **126**/-

*A rug is such an essential that it should be part of the equipment of the car.
The best type is rubber lined and, therefore, waterproof on the outside: wool
lined inside… It should not be less than 5ft in width and, if a foot wider,
can be tucked comfortably round both driver (who should sit on one edge to
prevent it fouling the gear levers) and passenger.*

How to Drive a Light Car or a Cyclecar by the staff of
The Light Car and Cyclecar, 1917

For full all-weather protection, though, combining moisture resistance
and warmth, the motoring gent should perhaps opt for the Waterproof
Foot Muff Apron as advertised in 1902 *Autocar Magazine*. This slinky
leather all-in-one (**Fig. 19**) keeps the driver dry and snug all the
way down to his extremities. A note of caution however – it is not
recommended if you are driving a car that comes with foot pedals.
In this situation it may well be inclined to compromise your driving
abilities, placing you in an awkward situation akin to trying to play
Rachmaninoff on the piano forte whilst dressed in a sleeping bag.

CHAPTER FOUR

FELLOW
ROAD USERS

COMRADES OF THE ROAD

Having passed his driving test, the novice motorist commonly experiences an all-consuming lust for acquiring his own vehicle and an hysterical urge to launch himself upon the open road. After all, what was all the expense, time and humiliation of learning to drive about if not the right to disport oneself on the highway in a huge shiny bullet of steel, laughing in the face of danger, whizzing around corners and menacing pedestrians? But the red-blooded acolyte of asphalt would do well to think again – and think again sharpish.

The public highway is not your personal and private racetrack. From the moment you trundle out of your drive you will be joining a society, a society of fellow motorists. Especially in towns and cities, where traffic volumes are obviously denser, you will be entering the equivalent of a gargantuan game board: a frighteningly complex game comprising the principles of billiards, chess, poker, the Rizla game and hunt the

Fig. 1 It pays to be polite to your fellow motorists. Remember: 'Every conceivable kind of person drives a car'.

slipper. You should not assume that fellow players are going to be imbued with the same calm, beauteous light of reason that you are:

> *The first and most important rule for the learner to absorb and never forget is this: Always assume that the other people you meet on the road, whether they are walking, driving either horses or motor cars, or bicycling, are fools; and that they are probably going to do something idiotic which will endanger your life as well as their own.*
>
> John Prioleau, *Motoring for Women*, 1925

Just as it sinks in that full enjoyment of your vehicle may be hampered by a mass of humanity who are two forks, three spoons and a fish knife short of a canteen of cutlery, then the full horror of what you must contend with will hit like the second wave of a tsunami.

> *Every conceivable kind of person drives a car* [**Fig. 1**] *– not only normal, but permanently or temporarily abnormal people: men and women with bad eyes, morons, thrill-seekers already arrested for recklessness, drunks, near-drunks, criminals in stolen cars, people tired to the point of collapse and half asleep at the wheel, nervous old ladies, rash and over-confident youths, motorists with headaches, sick people, drivers who have already killed or maimed somebody.*
>
> Richard Alexander Douglas,
> *Common Sense in Driving Your Car*, 1936

> *Temperamental personalities can only account for the extraordinary conduct of some motor drivers, who seem to have no faculty for observing the presence of danger, which causes them to become exceedingly reckless. Drivers of this type continue to be a source of danger to themselves and other road users, until they have been mixed up in an accident, which brings them to their senses and, it is to be hoped, produces a permanently sobering effect. Hairbreadth escapes are no use whatever as object lessons to such drivers, a real smash is the only thing that has any lasting results... Another type of*

person who takes some time in becoming a proficient driver is he who thinks very slowly and acts with corresponding deliberation. When the engine of a car is going round at about two thousand revolutions per minute, it is not easily controlled to the best effect by the person whose thoughts mature at a very much slower rate of speed.

Richard Twelvetrees, *All About Motoring*, 1924

Like the combined casts of *One Flew Over the Cuckoo's Nest, Freaks* and *Death Race 2000*, fellow motorists should be approached with extreme caution, but, as a gentleman, one should err on the side of charitable thought and, at first at least, give this shower of dangerous misfits the benefit of the doubt. Luckily, the size of our road network and the multitude of drivers means that the number of madmen on the roads is diluted by those of a saner persuasion. It is sometimes possible to drive for minutes, sometimes hours, without encountering a psychopath or imbecile, so the beginner should relax a little and embrace the camaraderie of the wheel. A cheery wave here, an encouraging toot-toot there go a long way to calming the savage breast. As time goes by and experience increases, the swiftly passing mass of motorists will start to disentangle and come into focus as specific types and groups.

THE LADY MOTORIST

Whilst having the utmost respect for the ladies, the motoring gent may well find that they are the first individual group of motorists that mark themselves out as worthy of his critical attentions.

Women drivers, from whom the world expects a pleasing countenance, are the worst offenders. The average woman, whether from self-consciousness or a nervous indulgence in a fierce joy, drives far too fast for real pleasure, and if a mirror on a dashboard reflected her driving expressions it is safe to say she would be very considerably surprised. [**Fig. 2**]

How to Drive a Light Car or a Cyclecar, by the staff of
The Light Car and Cyclecar, 1917

Indeed, there is something about the nature of velocity that acts directly on a lady driver's nervous system, causing her to grimace horribly. Even if she is able to suppress such facial distortions, there is no disguising the fact that an inexperienced female motorist often drives in a very different manner to her level-headed male counterpart.

The haughty-looking woman who sweeps along on the crown of the road as if it were a private path for herself alone, drives round corners without a warning signal, pulls up sharp without announcing her intention to do so, and refuses to make way for a car behind, in all probability does all this from sheer ignorance. If she could hear only a few of the comments which are passed on her behaviour by experienced witnesses, she would, being a sensible woman, mend her ways very quickly.

John Prioleau, *Motoring for Women*, 1925

Fig. 2 The dreadful facial contortions of a woman behind the wheel are a source of considerable grief to the gentleman passenger who regards the beauty of the female countenance as the very bedrock of Art.

Despite the unfortunate shortcomings of the incompletely tutored female motorist, it is, given time and patience, perfectly possible for a woman to become a very accomplished driver, changing gears remarkably smoothly and efficiently turning the wheel with her daintily gloved hands. After a while, her abilities behind the wheel will be virtually indistinguishable from those of her male colleagues – with possibly one small caveat:

> *There are certain situations in which one finds it impossible to concede that the average lady driver is the equal of the average male. The whole of the conditions referred to may be summed up in the one word "emergencies". Many ladies are really excellent drivers, thoroughly capable in every way, accurate in their gear changing, considerate for their cars, and with a due appreciation of the implied trust which they bear when driving...*
>
> *It is, however, on the odd occasion of the emergency that the lady driver is not likely to act with precision and, above all, absolutely instantaneously. Really this charge, whether admitted or denied, should not be looked upon as anything derogatory to the fair sex; it is merely a matter of Nature's ordinances, and with these we have no quibble.*
>
> How to Drive a Motorcar,
> by the staff of *The Motor*,
> 1920

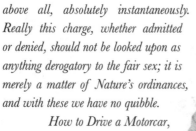

Fig. 3 Dealing with domestic grime. By far the best apprenticeship for the aspiring lady motorist.

So there we have it. There is little purpose in arguing with the voice of an expert, but perhaps we can even things up a little by noting that the male of the species is not immune from faults of his own. The gentleman driver may at times tend to show off behind the wheel, ostentatiously exhibiting his prowess under pressure and taking testosterone-fuelled risks that can put both him and his passengers under considerable threat of harm. Furthermore, despite her innate biological drawbacks, the lady can sometimes bring qualities to driving a motor vehicle that a man may lack. This will become particularly apparent with cars of an earlier construction where oil leakages and surplus grease are more in evidence than they are in modern vehicles.

I have no doubt as to the ability of the intelligent woman to become a perfectly efficient motor woman. Woman is far less afraid of dirt than man. She deals with it. [**Fig. 3**]

John Prioleau, *Motoring for Women*, 1925

It is at least reassuring to know that a lady's domestic duties can be used as invaluable 'transferable skills' when she decides to take to the open road.

THE LEARNER DRIVER

We have already tackled the intricacies of learning to drive in Chapter One, but *being* a learner driver and having to *deal with* learner drivers on the public highway are two very different things.

Novices will very quickly attract attention to themselves by their astounding array of idiotic shortcomings – stalling at traffic lights, grinding gears, performing 11-point turns and generally making a ruddy nuisance of themselves. It is an unspoken convention of the road that if one should ever find oneself hindered by their antics, the experienced driver should show solidarity with their plight and give encouragement for their endeavours by a cheery and repeated blasting of the horn.

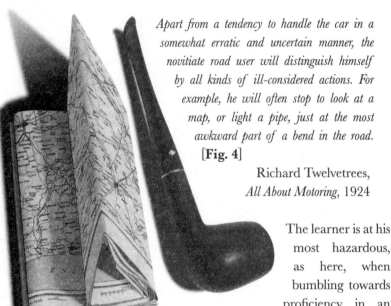

Apart from a tendency to handle the car in a somewhat erratic and uncertain manner, the novitiate road user will distinguish himself by all kinds of ill-considered actions. For example, he will often stop to look at a map, or light a pipe, just at the most awkward part of a bend in the road.
[**Fig. 4**]

Richard Twelvetrees,
All About Motoring, 1924

The learner is at his most hazardous, as here, when bumbling towards proficiency in an unmarked vehicle. Surely it is not asking too much (naturally, once one has passed the test oneself) that all trainee motorists should

Fig. 4 Map and pipe – highly dangerous items best avoided by the trainee motorist.

be required to herald their approach, like lepers with their bells, by training in designated driving-school cars, adorned with humiliating illuminated plastic beacons. At least then, the experienced gentleman motorist would not be obliged to second-guess the presence of a learner driver by having to constantly listen out for the derisive reveille of impatient motor horns that pursue trainee motorists wherever they go.

CYCLISTS

If we are to believe a species of car enthusiast known as the Clarksonite Tendency, cyclists constitute the worst plague to afflict humankind since the combined visitations of locusts, boils and the death of the first born.

Whilst occasionally sympathising with this viewpoint, the gentleman motorist will swiftly find that his chief objection to modern cyclists lies not in anything to do with their roadcraft, but in their lamentably low standards of sartorial nous. If the modern cyclist looked a bit

Fig. 5

like this (**Fig.** 5) then the motorist might be a damn-sight more sympathetic towards him, but sadly modern mores seem to dictate that the bicycling fraternity should debase themselves with filthy man-made 'Day-Glo' fabrics fashioned into patently vulgar designs (**Fig. 6**, overleaf) and this is usually rounded off with headgear that would make Darth Vader blush at the thought of such millinery overstatement.

Other than their unsightly choices in the wardrobe department, cyclists can also offend other road users by their apparent belief that the laws of the highway are an inconvenient optional extra – and one which they generally prefer to opt out of. Jumping the lights, ignoring zebra crossings, terrorising OAPs on pavements or riding on the wrong side of the road, cyclists are the surly adolescents of the macadam. In the following extract a particularly lethal combination of gender and bicycle riding makes a seemingly innocuous and easily negotiated encounter into something potentially far more hazardous:

You are driving along a broad high road either in the centre or near the side when you see a presumably intelligent woman riding a bicycle on the off and wrong side. You sound your horn; she pays no attention. You sound it again, and she continues to bicycle as if there was nobody else in the world but herself. Do not imagine that she is going to stay on her wrong side. On the contrary, persuade yourself that just as you draw level she will be seized with panic and wobble across the road to her proper side in front of the car, and doing everything in her power to get run over.

John Prioleau,
Motoring for Women, 1925

Fig. 6 Not a pretty sight. The ill-judged outfit choices of the modern cyclist.

Indeed, sometimes it seems that cyclists have as scant regard for their mortality as a bankrupt lemming whose wife has just left him, taking the children and the contents of their joint bank account with her. At weekends especially, 'serious' cyclists come out in force, backs arched like riled cats, knees on a latitude with earlobes, little feet revolving 19 to the dozen, and all this purely for the pleasure of stretching their limbs, chafing their nethers and adorning their backs with road slurry. The gentleman is advised to give these misguided creatures a very wide berth indeed.

Unlike the motorist, the bike rider is not required to prove any level of proficiency before launching himself upon his vehicle. The danger increases several fold when encountering cyclists afflicted with various levels of physical infirmity:

> *Cyclists who are even only slightly deaf should fit a mirror on the handlebar of their machine (right-hand side) and very carefully align it to ensure a clear view of overtaking traffic. I remember some time ago, seeing a cyclist with a large white square of cardboard tied to his back with the words "STONE DEAF" painted on it. That man was very sensible and I would not hesitate to do the same thing myself if I were deaf.*
>
> R.M.T. Treeve, *Real Road Safety*, 1946

It may not be a bad idea if a law were passed that obliged all cyclists to wear signs on their backs briefly summarising their psychological make-up or current mood. Signs such as 'DANGEROUSLY PSYCHOTIC', 'HALF WIT' or 'UTTERLY BLOTTO' would at least give the motorist a fair approximation of how to deal with the approaching obstacle ahead.

PASSENGERS

Sometimes a driver can become so engrossed by the passing freak show outside his windscreen that he overlooks one particular vehicle user who invariably turns out to be more of a nuisance than all the others lumped together. The 'passenger' (or the enemy within) has more potential to unsettle a driver's equilibrium – and cause an array of problems ranging from petty irritation to roadside carnage – than almost any other habitué of the highway. Eating unpleasant-smelling snacks, insisting on listening to Chris de Burgh on the in-car audio system, recklessly swotting flies or unexpectedly vomiting into the ashtray, the passenger is a primed time bomb that may go off at any second. Of all sins, the very worst that a passenger can commit is an insistence on providing advice when it is perfectly clear that no advice is needed.

> *A passenger should never be allowed to caution the driver, to give notice of the presence of other objects in the road, or of dangers fancied or real. If it is necessary, the driver had better give up driving for the more he is counselled, the more uncertain he will become, and this advice related to the passenger, coupled with the assertion that the next time it occurs the whole turn-out will be put in the ditch, has the desired effect.*
> How to Drive a Light Car or a Cyclecar, by the staff of
> The Light Car and Cyclecar, 1917

The incessant stream of cautioning that issues from some rear seats might give the driver a sense of being repeatedly pecked in the back of the head by a colossal woodpecker. It doesn't help matters

Fig. 7

that the person doing the pecking is generally a relative or close friend whom one doesn't wish to offend by telling them in no uncertain terms to shut their ruddy trap. Other than threatening imminent disaster, as above, the driver may wish to try various passenger-calming measures such as handing around a bag of particularly chewy toffees, singing a soothing lullaby or, if all else fails, subduing the offending parties with judicious use of a bottle of chloroform and a handkerchief. For close family members, with whom you can possibly afford to be a little more frank, the no-nonsense solution in **Fig. 7** might be more effective. After a small amount of Pavlovian training, eventually the mere sight of a blank cardboard placard or raised hand alone should be enough to quell even the most garrulous of back-seat drivers.

Having full control over one's passengers is particularly important when dealing with members of the constabulary:

Passengers should be advised to hold their tongue in cases of emergency, when coming into conflict with the police, or in an accident. Men usually do, but women give relief to their feelings by saying what is uppermost in their minds, and not, as a rule, a correct view of the situation. How often, therefore, after an accident, we read that the passenger made some unfortunate exclamation, such as "I knew you were going too fast" and its dire effect upon the already prejudiced magisterial mind.

How to Drive a Light Car or a Cyclecar, by the staff of
The Light Car and Cyclecar, 1917

With these words having been duly taken down and kept on record to be held against you at a later court appearance, you might start to wonder why on earth you ever decided to get behind the wheel of a motor car in the first place. Should you have a little spare cash to throw around, you may consider handing over the reins to an employee for a while, so that you might lean back and tackle the cocktail cabinet whilst he takes the flak for you.

THE CHAUFFEUR

If chosen wisely, your chauffeur is possibly one of the most agreeable 'fellow road users' you are likely to encounter, absolving the gentleman motorist not only from the daily stresses of driving his car, but also allowing him to indulge in his favourite hobbies, i.e. ladies and gin, without any consequent diminishment in standards of road safety.

Like heavenly manna, chauffeurs are not as thick on the ground as they used to be, but if a gent can possibly stretch his finances to take on a full-time driver then he will reap the benefits a thousand fold. Not only does a liveried driver look mightily impressive to the neighbours (particularly if you happen to live in a down-at-heel semi in Penge), but a properly trained chauffeur will also double up as car washer and engine tinkerer. Add to this financial reckoning the parking fines you will inevitably avoid by getting him to slowly circumnavigate the Red Lion all afternoon, whilst you indulge in a first-class ploughman's and innumerable frothing pints of Shropshire ale, and he will have virtually paid his own wages.

In fact, a chauffeur's all-round usefulness can lead to his master taking him somewhat for granted:

> *People who are very careful of the coachman, and would never think of asking to go out more than twice a day, and that only on occasions, look on the unhappy chauffeur as a machine which is turned out for the day, and he is expected to be on duty from "early morn till dewy eve". A chauffeur is after all but flesh and blood, and the temptations of the public house to a tired man are very potent. He doesn't get his meals regularly, and he cannot sleep on duty, so that after some hours, if a cold and perhaps wet day, he may well be pardoned if he takes something to refresh and invigorate him. It would be well for employers to think a little of the paramount importance of a chauffeur being absolutely sober, and it would be humane and kind to remember that he feels hunger, cold and thirst just as much as his employer.*

Lady Jeune, Autocar magazine, 1902

As the main purpose of employing a chauffeur in the first place is to be able to partake freely of the grape and grain without any subsequent unpleasantness with the forces of law and order, then the idea that you may drive your employee to drink through thoughtlessness and neglect is shocking to the compassionate master. Go out of your way to make your driver feel comfortable in his quarters, even if they do happen to be a hastily converted garden shed, and never overburden him with inessential duties. By the same token, your chauffeur should be careful not to overstep the mark on his side of the bargain:

> *The greatest stumbling block is perhaps familiarity. The master does not like to be spoken to, especially before friends, in words that only want, perhaps, "old chap" added, to make a sentence that the driver might use to his dearest friend.*
>
> 'A Four-Inch Driver', *The Chauffeur's Companion*, 1909

Precisely so. Nobody likes an over-familiar underling (**Fig. 8**). It is best, under the circumstances, never to address him by anything other than his surname and when addressing him, by dint of focusing your vision on the intersection between his nose and monobrow, never actually meeting his gaze. This is a commonly employed tactic when dealing with staff and is designed to undermine a chauffeur's natural cocksureness by giving the impression that you are actually engaging with him eye to eye whilst simultaneously instilling in him some strange lingering doubts.

Fig. 8 The unpleasantly chipper visage of an over-familiar chauffeur. A gentleman's driver should exhibit due deference, stopping just short of abject servility.

DRIVER SPOTTER:
AN 'AT-A-GLANCE' GUIDE

The Gentleman
This man has done his research. He is an aesthete of the asphalt and advertises the fact by wearing a sturdy pair of flying goggles and by clenching a briar in his mandibles. A thick carapace of brilliantine is used to neutralise the otherwise catastrophic effects that G-force can wreak on a man's coiffure.

The Poseur
At first glance this fellow might seem to epitomise the suave gentleman motorist, but to the trained eye there are a number of telltale signs that mark him out as a fake. The stretch-fit polo neck is at best a dubious item of clothing, but coupled with the nautical insignia on his breast pocket which relates to no recognised motoring or yachting club, and a blazer made entirely of Crimplene, it singles this chap out as wholly beyond the pale.

The Sunday Driver
Those who take their cars out for 'a spin' only at weekends are a varied bunch. One branch of the genus is the 'funny little man' who trundles along in his Hillman Imp at speeds rarely exceeding 18 mph. Fortunately for him, his membership of the Aberystwyth Swingers' Club stipulates no specific time of arrival.

The Ladies Who Lunch

A sight that strikes a cold dread into the heart of any gentleman motorist is that of a car on the road ahead of him seemingly on autopilot, as its driver and front-seat passenger animatedly discuss items of random tittle-tattle. That those who are usually guilty of such a crime are of the female persuasion will come as no surprise to the experienced motorist. Cheap gossip, fashion hints and talk of kittens have no place at the business end of a speeding motor vehicle.

The Old School

Reeking of old leather, gun smoke, horse manure and the blood of slaughtered animals, this fine venerable gent personifies the country idyll that many middle-class city folk aspire to. If only they knew that his vintage Bentley was actually purchased on the back of converting 240 acres of his inherited estate into the Valhalla Retail Pleasure-Dome Experience.

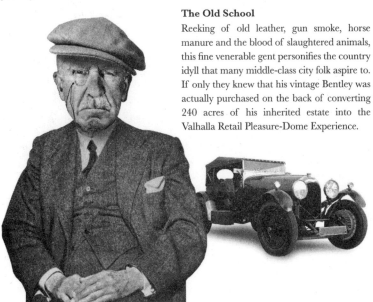

The Road Hog

Some fellows clearly believe that the open road is their personal, private property. Jumping queues and weaving in and out of traffic, this caddish oaf has allowed his Triumph Stag to fill him with so much hubris that in attempting to buy himself out of trouble he is actually purchasing a one-way ticket to a date in court and social ostracism.

The Travelling Salesman

With his perma-tanned flesh and a flashy suit hanging in the back of his VW Passat, this monstrous fellow marks himself as an arriviste. An ability to earn £80,000 a year without the aid of an Oxbridge education or influential relatives demonstrates his complete disregard for seemliness and convention.

The Family Man

The glories of Great British family life are the backbone of our society and an institution to which many a young fellow will turn when he has grown bored of living like a student, subsisting on kebabs and beer, and sleeping in gutters. That is, of course, until half-term holidays come around. At times like this, a young married man's fancy lightly turns to thoughts of days of yore, kipping face down in a skip outside the Railwayman's Arms in East Acton.

The Intercontinental Lorry Driver

Spending weeks alone on the road has put this fellow's grasp of reality so out of kilter that he no longer seems aware of the expected norms of sartorial finesse and personal grooming. No matter how full of rough-hewn charm he may be, his tufty mutton chops and Rockabilly quiff would not hold him in good stead if he were ever to submit an application for membership of the Sunningdale Golf Club.

The Boy Racer

Don't let the fresh face fool you. This half-crazed 'homie' has had his life hijacked by listening to 'hip hop' music, drinking caffeinated energy drinks, cruising for bootylicious babes and revving his engine unnecessarily in his parents' drive. He will surely be Bourton-on-the-Water's public enemy number one once he has saved up enough pocket money to take his driving test.

The Little Old Couple

At a cursory glimpse, passing motorists may be forgiven for assuming that they had just sighted the ghost car of Bridlington or witnessed the filming of a low-budget remake of *Herbie*. But taking a second look, a seemingly driverless vehicle is far more likely to be the domain of a little old couple, who, through a combination of calcium depletion and muscle wastage, no longer find it as easy to see out of the windscreen as they might have done in their youthful days.

The White Van Man

This cheery cove may give the impression of avuncular bonhomie but put him behind the wheel of a transit van and he instantaneously becomes a speed-crazed lunatic. An addiction to video games makes him regard his steering wheel as a console and all pedestrians as flesh-eating zombies who must be destroyed.

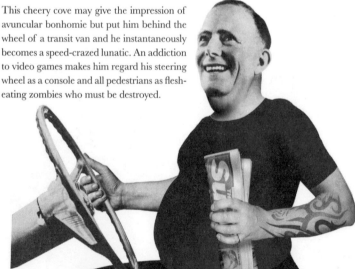

CHAPTER FIVE

RULES AND LAW ENFORCEMENT

THE LAWS OF THE ROAD

As soon as anything achieves mass popularity, whether it be tobacco, alcohol, gambling, recreational drugs, bear baiting, house windows or motor cars, then there will be a corresponding government department set up to regulate, tax or ban it, snapping at its heels like a demented terrier. Ever since the invention of the automobile, the powers that be have eyed it with suspicion and sought to legislate on its usage and, of course, milk it for every penny through the imposition of petty laws and taxes. Early motoring guides are full of gripes about magistrates, speed traps, the constabulary and a whole

Fig. 1 A poor naive young man shows off his newly acquired driving licence. Little does he suspect the expense and bureaucracy that lie ahead.

raft of legislation that seemed to be aimed solely at preventing the gentleman driver from having his full quota of unbridled fun.

For the gent, motoring is more of an art than a sport, and as with other art forms – such as free-form jazz, avant-garde painting and experimental theatre – he is rather inclined to tear up the rule book the moment it starts to get in the way of self-expression. To these ends, a gentleman only requires the official laws of the road as a rough framework or a palimpsest on which to carve his own artistic theories and extemporisations.

ESSENTIAL PAPERWORK

Once he has passed the driving test and been granted a licence (**Fig. 1**), the fledgling driver might be forgiven for assuming that he has reached the end of his dealings with authority, but nothing could be further from the truth. No sooner is Madam Government's truffling snout allowed to root around in the affairs of the motorist than she follows up her impertinence with a deluge of further paperwork accompanied by unreasonable demands for cash. At times it will feel that with every yard clocked up on the milometer there is a corresponding flow of cash out of one's bank account and into the government's rapacious coffers (**Fig. 2**).

The first expense he will encounter is probably car insurance. It matters not a whit that you have every confidence in your ability to

Fig. 2 With all the expense heaped upon the motorist he may gradually associate every yard with a haemorrhaging of his pockets.

swerve around objects at high speeds or that you have already paid handsomely, for a provisional driving licence, driving lessons and then a driving test, the government still insists that further outlay is necessary.

Car insurance is legally required of the motorist and it is primarily designed to cover the damage that his vehicle may chance to inflict upon those around him, but, more to the point, it can also be useful in guarding him from the harm that may be done to his vehicle, himself and his passengers. But before he gets too carried away with the shield of impunity that insurance cover seems to bestow, he should bear in mind that it does not give him automatic immunity from prosecution in the case of the running down of traffic wardens, sour-faced pedestrians or inconveniently positioned officers of the law. No, as you might imagine, there is even legislation to cover that sort of eventuality, and the sort of legislation that not only results in expense but the possibility of a lengthy prison sentence to boot.

The next insult to beset the driver is that of the MOT test. Actually standing for Ministry of Transport test, it was initially introduced in 1960. It is therefore something of a johnny-come-lately government extortion racket. Unless he is blessed with limitless funds, this annual test of roadworthiness is one of the great banes of the gentleman motorist's year. Favouring as he does a vintage car, any close scrutiny of the condition of his vehicle is likely to be beset with all sorts of misunderstandings, difficulties and, of course, expense. Although the gentleman, at best, has a rather ambivalent attitude towards dabbling in car mechanics (see Chapter Seven), from time to time throughout the course of a year he may be forced by circumstances beyond his control into attempting a working repair or two. It will only be when the MOT finally comes around that the full extent of such stopgap tinkering will come to light and all those pieces of the car that are held insecurely in place by judicious application of Blu-Tack, sticky tape, string or glue will suddenly come back to haunt him (**Fig. 3**).

Fig. 3 Beware – twine, sticky tape and household glue are frowned upon by professional mechanics as suitable materials for making permanent repairs to your vehicle.

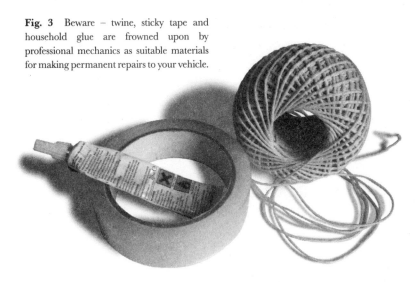

Then there is road tax or Vehicle Excise Duty, which is issued only after proof has been provided that a vehicle is insured and has a valid MOT. As luck would have it, current legislation stipulates that vehicles of pre-1973 construction are exempt from road tax charges, and as few chaps of discernment would deign to drive a car constructed *post*-1973 then at least in this one small respect the law of the realm seems to be firmly on the gentleman driver's side.

SPEED

Even from the earliest days of self-propelled road transport, when oldfangled steam- and hydrogen-powered machines still held sway over the public highway and Mr Karl Benz's newfangled motor car was no more than a glint in his eye, the heinous sin of speeding was already uppermost in the thoughts of local authorities hell-bent on pooping the party. Upsetting simple folk, causing apoplexy in port-soaked old majors, and quite literally scaring the horses, early automobiles represented a threat not only to life and limb but to the vested interests of the established transport structures too:

In 1865 an Act was passed: this was known as the "Red Flag" Act, and was one of the most disgusting ever put on the statute book in the history of our country. Toll owners, railway companies and home interests conspired to give the steam car a death-blow. The maximum speed was limited to four miles an hour in the country and two miles per hour in town, and each car had to be preceded by a man with a red flag. [**Fig. 4**]

John Harrison, *The Boy's Book of the Motor-Car*, 1926

As the sort of speeds stipulated by the Act were barely faster than might be achieved by a particularly ambitious tortoise with an urgent appointment to keep, this didn't go down very well with a nascent motoring fraternity that was beginning to discover exactly what larks could be afforded by rampaging around the streets and frightening the horses, not to mention unsuspecting pedestrians. Happily the Locomotive Acts, as they were officially known, were substantially reformed in 1896 and cars were allowed to travel at speeds up to a heady 14 mph, which was good news for everyone – with the possible exception of that band of men who had

Fig. 4 The Red Flag Act – just one in a long line of asinine requirements ·sanctioned by the law.

carved out a career for themselves and raised a family on the proceeds of flouncing along the road carrying a gaily coloured hanky on the end of a stick.

Even today it seems that an overly large proportion of the laws of the highway are dedicated to curbing the speed at which a driver is allowed to travel. Even though, most of the time, this will feel like an attack on his fundamental human rights, it has to be reluctantly admitted that speed can have an alarming tendency to bring out the beast in a gentleman motorist, rendering him inordinately bright-eyed and bushy-tailed.

Very many drivers unfathomably appear to be in such frantic haste to cover the ground in front of them that the idea of driving at a reasonable and safe speed apparently seldom, if ever, occurs to them.

R.M.T. Treeve, *Real Road Safety*, 1946

Good driving is not necessarily fast, or what one might term spectacular, such as darting fearlessly in and out of traffic, and racing up to corners and swinging round them with screeching brakes.

L.V.E. Smith, *How to Drive a Car Correctly*, 1926

Both Treeve and Smith may have a point here. It is indeed true that 'reasonable and safe' speeds do have their uses and that blood-curdling velocity should not represent the entire gamut of a gentleman's motoring repertoire (although, if he wishes to err on the side of fun, then blood-curdling velocity has the edge). No, a gentleman is not a shallow fiend addicted to only one speed; so, for the purposes of practical day-to-day driving he will actually require two, namely a 'moderate tootle' or a 'fair old lick'. It is doubtful that he will need to experiment with a greater variety of speeds, given that they are carefully designed for the purposes of being seen by all or for getting from A to B as fast as is humanly possible. The moderate tootle may also be useful for assuaging the fears of nervous passengers:

A speed of 25 m.p.h. is as fast as a passenger usually wants to be driven. Some few glory in speed, of course, but speaking for the majority, it may be doubtful if driving at 30 m.p.h. or 40 m.p.h. does not put a serious nerve strain, not upon the driver, who knows intimately and instinctively, what dangers to expect and how to avoid them, but upon the passenger, who has no means of checking the speed. The constant nerve strain frequently brings on a headache or a pain just below the diaphragm, quite wrongly attributed to indigestion.

How to Drive a Light Car or a Cyclecar, by the staff of
The Light Car and Cyclecar, 1917

If the carpings of his passengers are not enough to moderate an overly enthusiastic motorist's speed, the authorities have designed an impressive array of measures calculated to dampen his fervour. Today, technology is embraced in the form of speed cameras and police traps employing radar guns and laser speed detection equipment in an underhand attempt to undermine the gentleman motorist's morale. These are reinforced by further methods including warning signs, police patrol cars and large lumps of macadam in the road known as speed bumps or sleeping policemen. A gent should do his best to rise above this constant onslaught, but it doesn't take a genius to realise that what he is really up against is blind avarice:

Trapping is too often carried on, not in the interests of public safety, but in order to bring revenue to a locality. Some of the Surrey benches are still far too fond of breaking one another's records for mulcting the maximum amount in fines from luckless motorists. Time, however, in its irresistible march forces the surrender of the crustiest of die-hards, and a new generation of magistrates is taking a saner view of the antiquated legal machine.

John Harrison, *The Boy's Book of the Motor-Car*, 1926

It seems that even if the motorist is born free, on today's roads, everywhere he is in chains.

DEALING WITH MEMBERS
OF THE CONSTABULARY

Sooner or later a gentleman's independent spirit is calculated to bring him into meaningful intercourse with members of the constabulary. Perhaps he will have been driving too fast on his way to a rendezvous at the Hellfire Club, or maybe taken the scenic route over a roundabout, or perchance driven the wrong way up a one-way street the better to appreciate the architecture, but there is very little point in trying to explain such concepts to an officer of the law who has just flagged you down with a look of menace in his eyes.

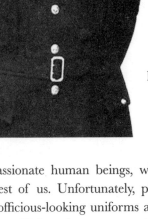

Fig. 5

By and large policemen (and policewomen for that matter) are normal, kindly and compassionate human beings, with desires, hopes and dreams like the rest of us. Unfortunately, place otherwise normal human beings in officious-looking uniforms and ill-fitting shoes and their personalities are likely to become every bit as pinched and ugly as their bunions.

When approached by an officer of the law it is terribly important not to seem at all cocky or frivolous. Wind down your window to reveal an expression of wide-eyed bemusement tinged with fear. If possible, remove yourself from your vehicle and assume a slightly hunched gait that will make the policeman feel a little more at ease with his social inferiority. On no account regard the situation as an opportunity for play. Lazily lowering the window of your vintage Bentley and greeting your interlocutor with a salutation ending in 'My Dear' or intoning some cod-Shakespearean phrase such as: 'How dost thou fare, Sweet Knight, 'pon this propitious dawn?' cannot be recommended under any imaginable circumstances. As with border control guards and tax inspectors, policemen should never be assumed to possess much by way of a sense of humour.

It goes without saying that no matter how plucky your citing of the Universal Declaration of Human Rights in defence of your entitlement to freedom of expression through the medium of creative driving, in a policeman's eyes such an argument will hold no water (**Fig. 5**). It is essential that you take your punishment unflinchingly. Stiff upper lip to the fore, greet any fine or summons with an abashed but faintly condescending smile. A gentleman does not beg or throw a tantrum, nor is it seemly to hang round a policeman's knees sobbing uncontrollably and fabricating some story about your ill mother or pregnant wife. Finally, it is only permissible for a gent to tell a policeman exactly what he thinks of him when he is back safely behind the wheel and some 150 yards away down the road.

HORN USAGE

So determined are the authorities to spoil a gentleman's pleasure that rules have also been set down that stipulate the exact manner in which the driver is allowed to use his motor horn. This is the most galling effrontery, especially if one happens to be the owner of a car of an older vintage equipped with a generous brassy hand hooter. Only the most self-controlled puritan could possibly resist the temptation of giving such an instrument a good old honk at regular intervals throughout a journey.

Today's Highway Code apparently stipulates that '*You MUST NOT use your horn when stationary in the road or driving in a built-up area between the hours of 11.30pm and 7.00am.*' Such a rule seems very flawed indeed, suggesting as it does that it is perfectly acceptable to sound one's horn during a gentleman's hours of sleep, which usually occur between 4am and noon. Equally, 11.30pm seems a preposterously early hour to impose a tooting ban and the further insistence that a vehicle should be in motion makes no sense whatsoever.

Fig. 6

The Department for Transport clearly hasn't thought this through sufficiently. How on earth is one supposed to summon one's lady-love to her moonlit balcony at three in the morning and at the same time avoid bumping into her disapproving parents without the aid of repeated blasting of a powerful car trumpet? In the light of this, perhaps councils should consider introducing a new road sign specifically designed to help a gentleman get his full quota of shut-eye (**Fig. 6**). Further suggestions for a range of similarly useful road signage are made later in this chapter.

Disappointingly, early motoring guides seem to side with the authorities with regard to horn usage:

A driver who tears through intersections, weaves in and out of traffic and relies on his horn to clear the way, should not be behind the wheel, but behind bars. Horn blowing is too often the raucous music of recklessness, the grunt of the savage armed with a two-ton club.

Richard Alexander Douglas,
Common Sense in Driving Your Car, 1936

The bad driver is he who blows the horn to order people out of the way instead of giving them warning and thinks that the horn takes the place of prudence.

Charles Baudry de Saunier, *The Art of Motor Driving*, 1909

The gentleman motorist would no doubt wish to enquire of Mr Baudry de Saunier, if one is not allowed to use one's horn then how on earth are errant pedestrians and other wrongdoers ever to learn the foolishness of their ways? Surely chivvying the wrong-headed with one's horn should be seen in the same light as administering a light flogging to a small child – a kindly act clearly designed to educate and instruct.

PARKING AND TRAFFIC WARDENS

Another area of conflict between the motorist and the authorities will occur in towns and cities where parking space is at a premium. Firstly, the motorist must ensure that he has parked his car correctly. As we saw in Chapter One, the acquisition of a dainty proficiency in reverse parking is now required as part of the driving test. Whilst this ensures that the positioning of your vehicle wins marks for style, it is of next to no help to the driver in determining the various insolent restrictions that have been imposed from street to street.

Councils are very keen on the regulation of parking because it is yet another easy means by which they can suck the motorist dry through the imposition of fees and fines for virtually anything and everything. A static vehicle sans driver is as easy to target as a mallard relaxing in a Parker Knoll recliner, which means that councils will immediately whip out their legislative blunderbusses and open fire.

The gent who parks his vehicle over the edge of a dotted line, or slightly impinging upon the pavement, or who resides a minute or two over a designated time period will be treated like a common criminal.

The sorry souls designated to police parking violations are known as traffic wardens (another merry introduction of the Road Traffic Act of 1960). As humourless as policemen but far more vindictive, traffic wardens prowl the streets in extraordinarily badly tailored items of clothing, but still manage to look a bit pleased with themselves (not a bad feat if you can pull it off). There is never any point in trying to win over the sympathy or affections of traffic wardens either through soothing words or gift items left under you windscreen wiper (**Fig. 7**). Instead, the gentleman motorist must treat their attentions as he would an over-familiar gnat, feel the pain, then swat them from his memory and venture forth into the rest of his day.

Fig. 7 As a rule, a traffic warden cannot be won over by small gift items left under one's windscreen wiper. This sniggery fellow will merely swipe your present and leave a penalty notice in its stead.

DRINK DRIVING

There was once a time in the dim and distant past (before the Road Traffic Act of 1930 to be precise) when the gentleman motorist would be reluctant to get behind the wheel of his vehicle without prior consumption of at least half a bottle of vintage port. The theory was that alcohol would inevitably serve to alleviate the awful tensions and vexations caused by interaction with fellow motorists, loosen up his limbs and thus make him a far more effective and competent driver. However, modern science, statistics and the law of the land now suggest that this viewpoint might be somewhat wide of the mark. It is therefore better to err on the side of sobriety or, if you are simply unwilling to countenance such a thing, then engage the services of a lady friend not as wedded to virulent liquor as you are.

If a gentleman is found to be tired and emotional behind the wheel, then he may be flagged down by an officer of the law and roundly humiliated by being asked to step out of his vehicle (a feat that may well be beyond his capabilities) and blow into an electronic gizmo designed to bleep idiotically and convert a glittering night out into a line of prosaic and sobering numerals. If he refuses such a request then it is possible he will be embarrassed even further by demands to open a vein or micturate into a receptacle back at the station. In an ideal world some sort of provision would have been made for a gentleman's sensibilities (**Fig. 8**).

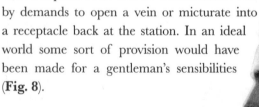

Fig. 8
The churchwarden/breathalyser hybrid – designed to put a gentleman at his ease when asked to give a breath sample.

TOWARDS A SYSTEM OF GENTLEMANLY ROAD SIGNAGE

The gentleman will no doubt have already gleaned all he ever need know about the UK system of road signage by having cursorily perused his Highway Code one wet afternoon prior to taking his driving test. It is therefore completely unnecessary to refamiliarise ourselves with the current range of dull pictograms here. However, modern signage does seem to be guilty of some serious oversights and unaccountably neglects to provide guidance for certain circumstances where it would seem judicious, not to say essential, to do so. Here are a few suggestions that would clarify matters no end and avoid a number of misunderstandings that often tend to occur on today's busy road network.

FAST FOOD VICTIMS AHEAD
(Black and white with red surround)
A warning designed to be placed on the approach to roadside fast food outlets. This sign alerts the gentleman motorist to the possible presence of slow-moving oafs drugged to the gills with monosodium glutamate and saturated fats meandering aimlessly about in the road ahead.

SNOOD ADVISORY NOTICE
(Black and white with red surround)
Warns of the possible need for a moustache snood. On certain windswept parts of the highway, especially on exposed coastal roads in Wales and Scotland, a gentleman ought to be informed if he is likely to encounter blustery side currents that might endanger a carefully sculpted facial hair statement.

POETIC REVERIES AHEAD
(Black and white with red surround)
There are some tracts of the British countryside that are so astoundingly beautiful that a driver may find himself overcome by lyricism, imperilling his life by drifting off into a state of semi-conscious hallucination. This sign counsels the driver to keep a tight rein on his daydreaming propensities.

STYLISH VEHICLES ONLY
(White on blue background)
There are certain localities that should be allowed to apply for restricted vehicular access status. These might include the Royal Crescent in Bath, particularly picturesque beauty spots or, for the bohemian gentleman, the segment of road outside his squat in a dodgy estate in Dalston.

NO BASEBALL CAPS
(Black and white with red surround)
Whilst the wearing of driving headgear is largely to be encouraged, it would be better fort the gent to forego it entirely if all he can muster is the sort of atrocity favoured by American sportsmen in the pursuit of baseball. Especially recommended for roads in the vicinity of cricket pitches.

FINISHING SCHOOL CROSSING
(Black and white with red surround)
The gentleman should be wary at all times of approaching hazards. By being forearmed on the approach to a finishing school he will be ready to take appropriate action, especially if a young lady of impeccable breeding happens to be sitting in a lonely fashion at the side of the road.

NO SPOILERS

(Black and white with red surround)

Denotes a complete ban on cars that have been defaced by the addition of unsightly spoilers. Should be sited on parts of the highway where aspirational vulgarians tend to lower the tone, such as the roads around lap-dancing clubs, lesser yachting marinas and financial institutions of the City of London.

OBLIGATORY SMOKING ZONE

(White on blue background)

Life can become a trifle tedious if one is compelled to transport individuals who do not share one's enthusiasm for tobacco products. Obligatory smoking notices defuse any petty argument regarding the rights or wrongs of tobacco consumption until the end of the zone has been reached.

SPOUSE DISPOSAL FACILITIES

(White on brown background)

The infernal yatterings of a judgemental spouse can lead to all sorts of problems including migraine, collisions and getting one's dander up. Designated spouse disposal zones would allow the driver to solve this problem efficiently and safely without cluttering up the roadside verge area.

ADVANCED WARNING OF DOFFING

(Black and white with red surround)

If the road ahead is rural, particularly narrow, and dotted with passing places, then it is essential for the gent to be forewarned that the journey ahead is likely to entail a good deal of doffing. He will then be able to gird himself for the extra strain he is likely to experience in his elbow region.

HAND SIGNALS

In these luxury days of traffic lights and electric car indicators we tend to forget that the motoring of the past demanded of the driver much uncomfortable flexing in the arm department. Happily, technology has largely freed him from having to utilise his hands and arms in mundane directional gesturing, allowing them instead to be used for other purposes, such as pipe smoking, hair combing, fiddling with the wireless or caressing a lady's perfectly formed knee. Nevertheless, it is still important to have a basic knowledge of hand signals just in case one's entire indicator circuits spontaneously phutter into inaction or one needs to amplify one's intentions to the colour blind, the foreign or the stupid.

As there is no danger of underestimating the rank idiocy of others, it is important to make one's intentions *very* clear.

> *There is nothing more absolutely bewildering than the sight of a hand making windmill motions, when the car containing the hand is in the middle of the road.*
>
> John Prioleau, *Motoring for Women*, 1925

> *The indefinite waving of a hand indulged in by many motorists is quite futile and is better omitted. The driver is the only person in the car who is authorised to signal at all, and passengers should refrain from interfering with his duties in this respect.*
>
> L.V.E. Smith, *How to Drive a Car Correctly*, 1926

For the purposes of clarity, the following pages outline the six essential hand signals that a gentleman will use for making his intentions clear on the public highway, although it should be noted that a gent's robust independence of spirit does mean that a certain leeway of interpretation should be brought to bear in deciphering their exact meaning.

No. 1
"I am going to TURN to my RIGHT."
or
"I am just about to slap the rump of
that attractive young FILLY on the
PAVEMENT."

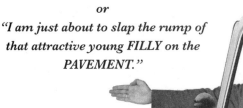

No. 2
"I am going to SLOW DOWN
or STOP."
or
"I am patting a small URCHIN on
the head as a reward for cleaning my
HUBCAPS."

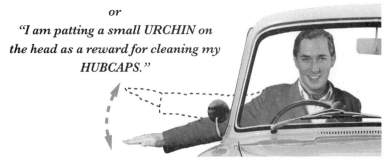

No. 3
"I am going to TURN to my LEFT."
or
"I am suffering from terrible CRAMP
in my RIGHT shoulder."

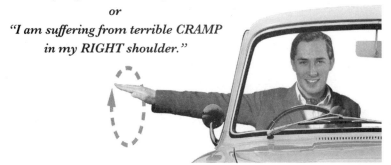

No. 4
"I detect a slight PRECIPITATION that bodes ill for this afternoon's fixture at EDGBASTON."

No. 5
"I am going to proceed STRAIGHT AHEAD."
or
"I find my PASSENGER is UNSIGHTLY and/or has dreadful HALITOSIS."

No. 6
"I am going to TURN LEFT but I have completely forgotten that my FIANCEE is sitting in the front passenger seat."

CHAPTER SIX

ETIQUETTE AND ROADMANSHIP

COURTESY BEHIND
THE WHEEL

Once he has been surfing the tarmac for a few months, the gentleman driver will gradually realise that merely scraping through his driving test or being on pleasant nodding terms with the laws of the highway does not a motorist make. To cut the mustard as a fully qualified automobilist not only involves knowing the basic rules of engagement, but also requires the application of various forms of driving etiquette and the acquisition of a mysterious commodity known as 'roadmanship'.

Roadmanship is not something that can be entirely learnt from manuals such as this, but, instead, like a deep-seated distaste for estate agents, it is an insight that slowly dawns with experience.

Fig. 1 Gazing at oneself for hours on end in a hand mirror should not be regarded as vanity in a gentleman but rather an essential preparation for engaging in the cut and thrust of the public highway.

To the gentleman driver, roadmanship is the nitty-gritty, the meat and two veg, the nub and the gist of the motorist's art, whereas etiquette is the caviar on his water biscuit, the lily in his buttonhole or the pearl in his oyster.

DEMEANOUR

The first concern of the all-round roadsman is to look convincing behind the wheel. He will already have progressed some way towards achieving this by following the dress code outlined in Chapter Three, but there is no point being suavely clad in your driving tweeds if your bearings and demeanour betray you as a rank dilettante. Looking nervous, flustered or utterly bewildered does not inspire confidence in passengers and fellow motorists, so before you take to the road several hours should be spent before the mirror perfecting a look of confident insouciance (**Fig. 1**). Experiment with clenching and unclenching your jaw, raising a quizzical eyebrow, ironically furrowing your brow or giving the merest hint of a knowing smile, before settling on your 'signature' combination of facial gestures (**Fig. 2**). At this point it is a good idea to seek out a second opinion. Make sure you try out your 'road face' on close friends before driving your vehicle. If they sink to their knees gurgling like a sewer pipe and wiping tears of mirth

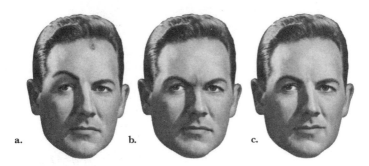

a.   b.   c.

Fig. 2 The Subtleties of Insouciance
(**a**) a quizzically raised eyebrow; (**b**) a furrowed brow or (**c**) the merest hint of a knowing smile – three techniques for giving the appearance of professionalism behind the wheel.

from their cheeks it is safe to say that you may have to reconsider your approach. Always bear in mind that what you fondly imagine to be the very spit of the inscrutable Mr Clint Eastwood in the closing scenes of *A Fistful of Dollars* may in actual fact be seen by others as the outward symptoms of acute constipation or some other medical condition.

> *As a rule, a look of set purpose on the face of a driver is an indication of nerve strain. Often it is produced by forcing the pace at a time and under conditions which call for alertness. Sometimes it is the result of sheer nervousness. It is accompanied by consciously holding the breath, and instead of a blow in the fresh air giving the driver a real fillip at the weekend, it sometimes has quite the opposite effect.*
>
> How to Drive a Light Car or a Cyclecar, by the staff of
> *The Light Car and Cyclecar*, 1917

If you don't happen to be a 'natural' when it comes to looking majestic behind the wheel then there might be nothing for it but to moderate the speed of your vehicle.

Fig. 3

> *As a means of cultivating an easy, graceful position at the wheel [**Fig. 3**], without facial distortions, a strictly moderate speed should be indulged.*
>
> How to Drive a Light Car or a Cyclecar, by the staff of
> *The Light Car and Cyclecar*, 1917

This may well be anathema to the sort of cove who judges his worth by the number of decibels he can squeeze out of his screeching tyres or, indeed, his screeching passengers, but sometimes sacrifices must be made for the sake of appearances, and for a gentleman of quality appearances should be *everything*.

SANGFROID AND COURTESY

Fig. 4

After perfecting the *look* of calm sophistication, a motoring chap must then develop suitable behaviour to match. It is the sacred duty of a gent to act as a beacon of civilised light that illuminates the lives of those around him. With the streets awash with petty provocation he will require nerves of steel to keep his head under such pressure.

> *Do everything in a cool, calm and deliberate manner, never get flustered, agitated or excited.*
>
> R.M.T. Treeve, *Real Road Safety*, 1946

> *It is very necessary to keep your temper when at the wheel. Even under the most trying circumstances bad temper is very futile and apt to lead to your behaving in a most indiscreet manner.*
>
> L.V.E. Smith, *How to Drive a Car Correctly*, 1926

The spectre of indiscretion is a continuous threat to a gent's *savoir faire*. Completely 'throwing a wobbly', swearing loudly, tearing chunks out of your hat with your teeth (**Fig. 4**) and jumping up and down until your face turns puce (clashing terribly with your eyes of azure) will not only lose you favour with passengers, but may also result in distress to passers-by, cause crying in infants, heart attacks in elderly matrons and spontaneous bowel evacuation in pet dogs, which isn't admirable by anyone's standards (with the possible exception of the adolescent fans of Mr Marilyn Manson). If a driver fails to keep his emotions under close restraint and starts to allow his passions to run away with him then in all likelihood he will begin to act up at each and every turn.

> *A driver shows his want of sangfroid by scolding the man in charge of a level crossing because he enforces the regulations, stupid though they may be; getting into a temper because there is a herd of cattle in the middle of the road (the motorist will never have the power to transform beasts into swallows which will disappear at the sound of his horn); saying nasty things to slow wagon drivers, sleepy country people and children who run about the road; replying to the insults of pedestrians; and getting irritated over a punctured tyre, a misfiring engine, or another thing that causes him temporary embarrassment.*
>
> Charles Baudry de Saunier, *The Art of Motor Driving*, 1909

As it escalates, such behaviour can develop into a condition known as 'road rage' or 'acting up like a real stinker'. Instances of this are increasingly making it into the headlines, where merely 'losing it' turns into something far more extreme and an enraged driver is not only moved to chew chunks out of his headwear but sometimes out of fellow motorists and members of the constabulary too. It would well behove any gent to nip feelings of this sort in the bud – street brawling has never been the domain of a gentleman, and may do irreparable damage to his trouser creases and his reputation (**Fig. 5**).

Sangfroid is naturally followed up with courtesy. Every opportunity should be taken to impress fellow road users with the depth of your generosity and decorum:

> *Good manners beget good driving. Nowhere is a gracious act appreciated, and a boorish act resented, more keenly than on the highway. When buying*

a ticket for the movies, one doesn't elbow one's way to the window ahead of all who are waiting in line. Why, then, should a motorist elbow his way through traffic, forcing everybody else to make room for him?

Richard Alexander Douglas, *Common Sense in Driving Your Car*, 1936

Drive always with courtesy. A car driver would not think of eating his meals like an uncouth savage, and yet many have manners when at the wheel which are despicable.

L.V.E. Smith, *How to Drive a Car Correctly*, 1926

Sadly, on the roads of today, the motoring equivalent of an eructating wild man is never too difficult to locate, but by ushering other vehicles before you and exhibiting grace in all things you will encourage fellow motorists to do likewise. When another car does make way for you or performs

Fig. 5 Episodes of road rage are unbecoming to a gentleman. Unlike an impressive collection of duelling scars, a black eye and split lip are not injuries a man of quality should aspire to.

some other helpful act it is only polite that you should acknowledge such assistance. This is sometimes done by the raising of a hand or a flash of the headlights, but a more elegant technique is a brisk doff of one's hat. Sadly, doffing is not seen as frequently on our roads as it once was, but it is high time there was a concerted campaign to reinstate such practices. Perhaps adding doffing technique to the driving test is something that ought to be considered with the utmost urgency. Doffing opportunities occur at passing places on narrow country lanes, or when generosity is shown in giving way at a traffic intersection, or where the thoroughfare is partially obstructed. However, it may also be used as a reward, perhaps to congratulate another motorist on the shininess of his chrome or the suaveness of his driving technique, or to acknowledge the fact that he is driving exactly the same model and year of car as you are. Most doffs should err on the side of minimalist. Whilst a grand flourishing doff of the sort one might expect from a French duke may sometimes be used between best friends in a jocular context, between strangers it should merely consist of an elevation of barely two inches clear of the cranium and should be clipped and business-like in movement (**Fig. 6**).

DEALING WITH PEDESTRIANS
AND OTHER IRRITATING OBJECTS
CLUTTERING UP THE PUBLIC HIGHWAY

In the hit parade of motoring irritants, pedestrians are ranked barely a notch lower in irksomeness than car passengers. Even if it is possible to vet, select or debar passengers, the sad reality is that once they have gained admittance to your vehicle it is very difficult to dislodge them. Pedestrians at least have the common decency to reside on the exterior side of the windscreen, making it much easier to a) avoid meeting them, and, if all else fails, b) repel them with your bumper. The only other thing that pedestrians have in their favour is that they provide a ready audience ideally situated to witness a gentleman's stylistic exuberances and devil-may-care antics. Without the perambulating

Fig. 6 Precise and proficient doffing.
The mark of a true gentleman.

hoi polloi, the driver would have only fellow motorists to impress and would never experience the profound satisfaction of inspiring not only awe and appreciation, but (if he applies the correct principles of car selection and driving technique) abject envy and fear too.

Like unwashed peasants loitering without the ramparts of a medieval castle, pedestrians seem to have no earthly purpose other than to make the thoroughfare look untidy. Their intellectual capacities and attitude may well come under scrutiny too:

> *From the driver's seat, pedestrians seem to have somewhat the same intelligence as the average sheep. Who has not watched them dart from behind parked cars, cross between intersections or wade into a stream of traffic against the red light? Their utter indifference to the value of their own lives is as astonishing as it is tragic.*
>
> Richard Alexander Douglas, *Common Sense in Driving Your Car*, 1936

I have sometimes seen pedestrians saunter across a road, in front of oncoming traffic and not even make a reasonable attempt (as they undoubtedly should) to cross without causing vehicles to stop, when they could easily have done so, the attitude adopted being that they (the pedestrians) had as much right on the road as the vehicle and its driver.

R.M.T. Treeve, *Real Road Safety*, 1946

After spending some time behind the wheel of a car dealing with this sort of effrontery, it is not surprising that the harassed gentleman motorist may start to regard the pedestrian with a certain level of dismissiveness or even contempt (**Fig. 7**), but he would do best to pull himself up short in these feelings. The burden of a gentleman's civilised heart does of course require him to treat pedestrians with a modicum of compassion (a compassion that is barely deserved, but nonetheless). There is an unspoken rule that stipulates that as long as a pedestrian stays where he or she ought to be – the pavement, designated crossings, in shops, on park benches or, preferably, in their own homes – then he must treat them with the utmost grace and courtesy. If, on the other hand, they stray but an inch into the penalty area otherwise known as the road, then they have voluntarily declared themselves 'sitting ducks'. But before you slam your foot down on the accelerator and take aim, you should bear in mind the possible consequences of your actions.

To make pedestrians scamper out of your way is dangerous. You may misjudge their agility. Or they may not scamper. It is also impolite. If the chasing of pedestrians is to be excused as a boyish prank, that type of boy should be removed from the one place where he obviously doesn't belong – behind a steering wheel.

Richard Alexander Douglas, *Common Sense in Driving Your Car*, 1936

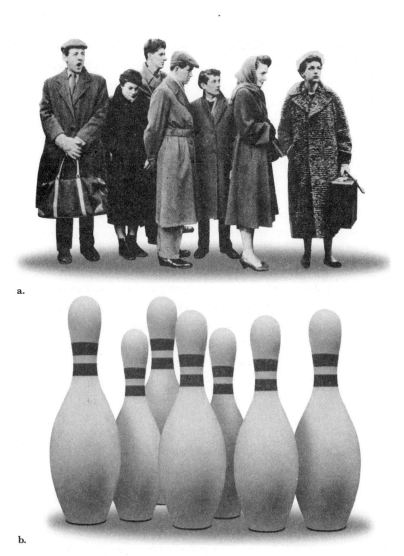

a.

b.

Fig. 7 A motorist, jaded by having to deal with the antics of pedestrians, may gradually develop a condition known as 'courtesy fatigue'. In the tertiary stages an innocuous queue of people at a bus stop (**a**) may take on the aspect of a row of tantalising skittles, lined up and waiting to be toppled (**b**). The gentleman driver affected in such a manner is advised to stop his car, wind down his window and take several deep breaths before continuing his journey.

Possibly a step too far, but as with the grouse when in season, those who decide to travel by foot should be given a sporting chance lest you end up answering for your actions in court or even in chokey. Here, for example, is a scenario where trying one's best to encourage an old lady in her passage across the high street with an innocuous and kindly toot-tooting of your horn may have unforeseen consequences, for both you and the old lady, and for the carriage work of your vehicle.

> *There are occasions when it is best not to sound the horn. For instance an old woman may be walking across the road and there is plenty of room for you to pass silently behind her. Should you sound your horn she maybe startled and, losing her head, may run back under your wheels instead of proceeding peacefully across to the other side.*
>
> British School of Motoring, *How to Drive a Car*, 1950

It is not only the elderly who exhibit a wanton unpredictability in the face of oncoming traffic. Young mothers can often be seen using their

Fig. 8 A hormone-crazed young mother pushes her pram haphazardly into the road whilst looking the wrong way for oncoming traffic.

LOOK OUT, MADAM!

perambulators as exploratory probes, pushing them out into the road in order to gauge whether it is safe to cross, or as an instrument for barging their way through rush-hour traffic. Naturally, it doesn't help matters that, suffused with an overload of hormones after childbirth, ladies very rarely know their left from their right, making them even more hazardous to approaching motorists (**Fig. 8**). It is essential that the gentleman driver always keeps a wary eye out for the aberrant antics of motherhood.

Children are another challenge to a gentleman's driving skills. At all times he must be vigilant for the harbingers of approaching youth. A gaily hued bouncing ball that abruptly appears from behind a parked car should be regarded with suspicion as it usually portends a gaily hued bouncing child in its wake. These days other telltale signs of the presence of youngsters at play will include dried peas ricocheting off your bonnet, exploding paint-ball pellets obscuring your windscreen and items of household furniture set ablaze in the middle of the highway. It is not always recommended to slow down in such circumstances. Stopping and attempting to be kindly to misbehaving children will either result in a chorus of 'Push off, grandad' or, even worse, being mistaken by local vigilante groups as a predatory pervert. No, indeed, the only option is to slam your vehicle into reverse or (if you are capable of such a thing) perform a handbrake turn and flee that particular vicinity as fast as is humanly possible.

In practice, the gent behind the wheel does his best to be cordial and indulgent, even with the most errant of pedestrians, and especially if they happen to be juvenile, old, infirm or, of course, a pretty young lady with shapely calves. However, the motorist's contract of trust with the public may be suspended in one or two very specific instances. The first of these concerns the etiquette of puddle avoidance. Courtesy usually dictates that, no matter how tempting, the motorist should always refrain from deliberately spattering pedestrians by driving at high speeds through residual water and liquid mud at the side of the road. However, this rule is temporarily lifted when those in question happen to be engaged in activities of a criminal nature, such as rioting, looting or queuing to buy tickets for a Coldplay concert. In such cases, a good drenching should be seen as a kindness and may act as a much-needed corrective to socially unacceptable modes of behaviour.

A similar suspension of the rules of etiquette comes into effect when encountering so-called squeegee merchants at traffic lights. The sight of one of these miscreants lumbering towards you carrying a bucket of tepid filth and with an expression of set purpose on his weathered features is apt to chill the soul of the owner of a highly polished vintage vehicle. There is no truly satisfactory way of dealing with such people. A frantic waving of the arms in the hope of wafting them away rarely works and a gent's only hope lies in threatened violence or, failing that, disorientating them with verbal obfuscation. An old service revolver or swordstick will generally make your objections plain, but they may be frowned upon by the constabulary. A less prosecutable course of action is to confuse your assailant by loudly intoning some Dada poetry ('Ursonate' by Kurt Schwitters is a perennial favourite) or a 15th-century Satanic incantation. With luck, filled with mystification and fear, he will gradually back away from the vehicle just in time for the lights to change.

ENCOUNTERING PETS, LIVESTOCK AND WILDLIFE

If the pitfalls of dealing with pedestrians are apt to try a gent's patience then he should seriously gird his loins for the challenge of his first encounters with animals and wildlife on the road.

During the day in the urban environment his two main concerns will be cats and dogs. If a domestic pet happens to charge headlong into the road in front of you, before panicking and flinging the steering wheel hither and thither in a desperate attempt to avoid a collision, be careful to learn the essential difference between our feline and canine friends:

Now a dog is an animal that can be "dodged" on the road with a fair amount of success, but many a driver has met with a bad accident through attempting to do so... there is a danger in that hitting a dog a glancing blow with a front wheel the steering will be deflected, possibly with serious results... Cats should never be "dodged". The chances are a thousand to one, even if puss is right in the path of one's wheels, that she will easily avoid them but if the driver swerves the odds are that the cat will be run over.

How to Drive a Light Car or a Cyclecar, by the staff of
The Light Car and Cyclecar, 1917

In possession of this knowledge, the gent can cheerily ignore cats on his travels and concentrate on being considerate and courteous to dogs instead. Even caddish drivers with caninocidal tendencies (**Fig. 9**) ought to be circumspect when it comes to accidentally or intentionally running dogs down in the street.

Fig. 9 Targeting harmless animals with your vehicle is a hobby only indulged in by the lowliest of cads.

I would remind drivers who are sufficiently hard hearted and badly educated to drive over a dog as they would a rag, that the dog possesses enough inertia to cause a catastrophe. It often happens that when overtaking vehicles dogs jump out from underneath and are run over because the drivers do not give them time to save themselves. In order to give pause to such drivers I hope that if they should be touring in the Upper Savoie they will see in a certain village a memorial plate which was put there to commemorate an automobile accident which took place four or five years ago. A motorist thought it good sport to run over any dogs he encountered on

the road, and one day he came across a dog which accompanied a cart.
He ran over it as usual. The steering wheels deflected, and the brute smashed
his head against a house.

Charles Baudry de Saunier, *The Art of Motor Driving*, 1909

In rural locales, dogs and cats combine forces with various farmyard animals in a veritable orgy of motoring inconvenience. If a gent's heart tends to sink at the sight of a squeegee merchant, then it positively plummets down his trouser legs and rattles around in the toes of his Tricker's at the approach of a herd of dull-witted Friesians urged on by a dull-witted farmer with a big knobbly stick. This plummeting sensation is likely to increase a thousand fold if you happen to be driving a 1938 Talbot-Lago T23 Goutte d'Eau Coupé by Figoni et Falaschi, the only compensation being that the vehicle's 'teardrop'

Fig. 10 A match made in hell – an unfortunate encounter between the sleek coachwork of a 1938 Talbot-Lago T23 Goutte d'Eau Coupé and a ruddy great Friesian cow. No good can be expected to come from this.

design will at least echo your own hot tears of frustration as a multitude of muck-spattered bovine legs scour your fenders with manure consommé (**Fig. 10**).

Similar vexation can be expected from flocks of sheep. Whereas the pedestrian can sometimes *seem* to have intelligence on a par with the average sheep, the average sheep is burdened with the *actual* intelligence of a sheep and, sadly, *all* of the time. A motorist caught up in an ovine deluge will have the sensation that he is adrift in a sea of woolly porridge, and a very unpleasant sensation it is too. In the cases of both cows and sheep, the gentleman motorist will do his utmost to keep out of the way of such abominations, but if the worst comes to the worst then he will adopt the same procedure previously recommended for the avoidance of children and, if he is sensible, will scarper from that particular vicinity *tout de suite*.

The final category of animal a gent will encounter on the highway is 'wildlife'. No matter be he in town or country, creatures of the wild seem to regard it as their God-given mission to lurch unannounced onto the public thoroughfare any time, day or night, wantonly mangling themselves in radiators, bumpers and under-chassis. A useful tip, particularly for the night-time driver on country roads, is always to travel in convoy. Current laws dictate that a driver accidentally mowing down pheasants (as opposed to peasants), grouse and other game birds is not allowed to profit from the collision by gathering up the carcass and cooking it, but the car behind you is legally permitted to do so. Whenever in the country, it is recommended to drive in a suitably swift sports vehicle equipped with a modified bumper (**Fig. 11**, overleaf). This should be followed by others of your party in a capacious hatchback or butcher's van. This way, you will be able to hold some stunning *soirées gastronomiques d'animaux tués par des voitures* without any shameful appearances before the magistrate. For those of a more adventurous palate, other items of run-over wildlife can be experimented with. There is no prouder moment for the motorist-chef than when he can triumphantly impress his guests

Fig. 11 An MGB sports car equipped with a specially modified game-bird bumper attachment. An essential accoutrement for the keen amateur chef.

with a 'road kill' creation based on Grimod de La Reynière's 1807 recipe for *rôti sans pareil* ('roast without equal') in which he might serve a badger stuffed with a fox, a squirrel, a hedgehog, a stoat, a garden warbler and a vole. For those with less time on their hands, a simpler, but creatively presented, wood pigeon and badger pie is a pleasing but easier alternative (**Fig. 12**).

PAYING ATTENTION ON THE ROAD

A good deal of roadmanship consists of keeping one's eyes peeled and developing an awareness of the constantly changing road conditions around you.

> *The driver should train his eyes to picture not only probabilities but also possibilities. Take the case of a pedestrian apparently wandering aimlessly in the centre of the road. Now, although it is done probably 99 times out of 100, and although one may advance sound arguments that it is excusable, nevertheless it should not, in point of fact, be argued by the driver that*

because he sounds his horn the said pedestrian will move to the side of the road. The trained eye naturally assumes the very strong possibility of such a thing happening, but has a glimmering vision as to the possibility of that person being deaf, hopelessly 'in the moon', stupid, or even drunk.

The Motor magazine, *How to Drive a Motorcar*, 1920

A considerate and well trained driver will be forever vigilant for those little telltale signs that herald the unexpected. The presence of an ice cream van at the side of the road will, of course, alert the driver to the presence of the youth or the sluggishly paced obese. Similarly, a semi-naked man clad only in a pair of socks and a balloon, clinging to a sapling on the grass verge, will immediately tell the driver that he is in the vicinity of a rugby club stag party and that there are almost certainly bound to be other similarly impaired imbeciles on the loose. The gentleman driver will cheerfully take all this in his stride. The challenges presented by all eventualities, from towed vehicles to slow-moving caravans, from plagues of migrating toads to escaped herds of wildebeest, must be one and the same to him. He should never drop his guard.

Fig. 12

Everything conspires to divert your attention but nothing must be permitted to divert it. Not even the pretty girl seated beside you, not the friend you see on the sidewalk, not the views, home numbers, not any of the countless objects that pass before your eyes – not even the explosion of a bomb in a car behind... The King of Belgium was motoring one day with the Queen. Suddenly his car left the road and plunged down an embankment. He was injured, she was killed – all because he looked at a map! Unless you are creeping on an empty road, there is neither space nor time to look at a map, tune the radio, light a cigarette, put on gloves, fight insects, or do anything else that takes your hands off the wheel, your eyes off the road or your mind off the job of driving.

Richard Alexander Douglas, Common Sense in Driving Your Car, 1936

In these vulgar times there are even more opportunities for a crash to occur. Dabbling with mobile phone technology, eating dreadful food obtained from so-called 'drive-thru' burger emporia and paying too close attention to satellite navigation systems aren't designed to keep your wheel rubber in firm contact with the highway.

CRASHING WITH PANACHE

If he drives on a regular basis, then sooner or later a gentleman is bound to drop his guard just sufficiently to find himself involved in some sort of collision. Usually this will be of a trifling nature, perhaps a mere matter of reversing into a brick wall or lightly running over a minor member of staff, but if the gent happens to be driving in springtime (possibly in conjunction with an unfavourable phase of the moon) and is accompanied by a beautiful young lady and/or a selection of spirited chums, then the possibility of a more serious outcome is increased considerably. A young man's desire to prove his mettle during the rutting season can cause him to become the sort of driver that he would usually claim to abhor.

That large class of drivers who are fond of 'putting on side' and for whom the greatest ambition is to do something clever, such as passing between two carriages with only a hair's breadth to spare, shaving the horses' noses, and appearing on the scene like an instrument of destruction which comes from no one knows whither and disappears in the dust.

Charles Baudry de Saunier, *The Art of Motor Driving*, 1909

Whilst such antics can never be condoned, if a young blade feels so utterly compelled by the dictates of Madam Nature to perform a breathtaking stunt, perhaps involving a series of swerves, a scattered church procession, roadworks, a spooked horse attached to a rag-and-bone cart, and 150 yards of burnt rubber and dazed pedestrians, he had better make sure that he is very certain of his driving technique (**Fig. 13**). The line between universal admiration and several years' imprisonment for manslaughter is a very slight one.

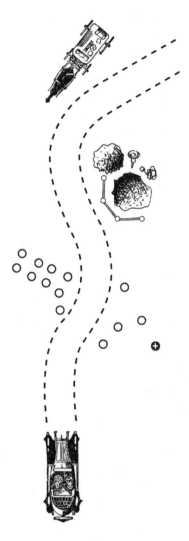

Fig. 13 Not recommended. The haphazard trajectory described by a young blighter seeking to impress his friends. Collision with a church procession, roadworks, and horse and cart are just narrowly avoided.

A better plan is to operate under the aegis of 'sensible driving' and wait for the road collisions to make their way to you. You can then acquit yourself admirably and impress your passengers by acting cool in a crisis. With luck, when a drama does occur, you will be able to manage the situation so well that in return for only glancing damage to your vehicle you win the opportunity to act heroically and look immensely impressive in front of your friends into the bargain.

Acting like a ruddy ass behind the wheel, then walking away from the consequent crash with but one brilliantined strand of hair out of place is rumoured to be one of the most delectable aphrodisiacs known to womankind. It is imperative that you use your new-found powers wisely. As you hurtle towards your fate, make sure to instruct your lady passenger in accepted 'crash etiquette'. Be firm and commanding:

> *It is not a bad idea to instruct a passenger on what to do in the unlikely event of an accident occurring. The check points to bear in mind are to jump clear only if the driver says so, and otherwise to brace the feet against the footboards, and protect the head from being thrown through the windscreen by placing a hand on the dash... If a collision with a solid body is inevitable, while doing everything to reduce the speed of the car, at the last moment grip the steering wheel firmly with both hands and steer it as straight as possible, cautioning the passenger to 'hold tight'.*
>
> How to Drive a Light Car or a Cyclecar, by the staff of
> The Light Car and Cyclecar, 1917

Should you find your vehicle brought to a halt in the village pond or a mosquito-infested ditch, calmly light up a pipe or cigarette, smooth back your locks and glance knowingly at your companion. If she is still a) in situ and b) breathing, say something immensely amusing like: 'If I had known we would be ending up in here, I would have brought my ruddy periscope!' and watch her heart turn to putty.

CHAPTER SEVEN

MAINTENANCE AND REPAIRS

ROUTINE MAINTENANCE

The early days of motoring were akin to a bold expedition into an unexplored continent: it was anyone's guess whether you could reach your destination and pretty much odds-on that you wouldn't return from your adventure entirely unscathed. In fact, most 19th-century cars seem to have been manufactured with hilarity aforethought and with reducing the yokels to giggling imbecility as one of their prime functions (**Fig. 1**):

> *There is nothing so wounding to the pride of a chauffeur and his master as a breakdown near London, where the disabled car is surrounded by a crowd of jeering and unsympathetic onlookers. The inhabitants of the town understand somewhat of the difficulties, and the sight is not an uncommon*

Fig. 1 Withering contempt and clay pipe brandishing – sadly not much more can be expected from unsophisticated wayside yokels.

Fig. 2

one, but to the country bumpkin the sight only fills him with unlimited amusement and food for chaff. "'E finds this so 'ealthy 'e's come again for a change of air", said one hodge to another last week on finding the same car in difficulties on the top of the same common where he had seen it the day before.

Lady Jeune, *Autocar* magazine, 1902

Thankfully, these days it is easier to avoid the sour provocations of country folk as more mechanically advanced models of car are available and they can be kept in good health with a simple regime of routine maintenance.

Most gentlemen will have mixed feelings about the prospect of sticking to a 'routine'. Of course there will be pleasant things like his habitual trip down to the tavern, turf accountant, tobacconist or mistress, but, there again, the term might conjure up onerous tasks such as visiting in-laws, chairing charity meetings or traipsing all the way upstairs to kiss one's offspring goodnight. But unless the gentleman owner wants his cherished Vauxhall Victor (**Fig. 2**) to rapidly revert to its component parts, and thence its chemical ingredients, then certain things have to be done to preserve its pristine condition.

First on the list is car washing. The cleanliness and shine of his car is often seen as a gentleman's badge of honour, and even though denizens of the countryside and the dangerously eccentric might insist that a substantial accretion of filth on a vehicle is in some way

Fig. 3 A filthy street urchin. It is no longer politically or socially correct to employ young children to perform menial tasks for derisory sums of money, unless of course they happen to be your own cherished offspring.

strangely admirable, such wayward thinking is usually frowned upon when driving in town:

A dirty car is an abomination, whether you are going to sell it or whether you are going to keep it.

John Prioleau, *Motoring for Women*, 1925

It may seem to the fledgling motorist that car washing is the second task Beelzebub invented after he came up with the exquisite torture of 'hoovering', and that is chiefly because it is. The experienced gentleman driver will do almost anything within his powers to lessen the burden of this irksome chore. There are certain technological ways of doing this:

Washing and cleaning a car is one of the tiresome and dirty jobs which deter many people who cannot afford a chauffeur from motoring. Chromium plating has largely eliminated the cleaning difficulties. For a small sum the motorist can have all the nickel and exposed parts of his car chromium-plated, and since rust cannot live on a chromium-plated surface, it can be kept at mirror-like brightness by the simple wipe of a rag.

Professor Archibald M. Low,
The Wonder Book of Inventions, 1930

Despite the wonders of chromium plating, car washing is clearly a mug's game; but still, many of questionable sanity seem to derive a grim satisfaction from it and are all too happy to parade their idiocy in their driveways on weekend mornings for all the world to see. The best way of avoiding such unpleasantness would be to get some member of the lower orders to wash the car for you, but sadly, due to complex social, political and economic reasons (with which we won't embroil ourselves here), it is no longer so easy to get street urchins, boy scouts or chauffeurs to co-operate with such strategies (**Fig. 3**). If you find yourself in straitened circumstances, the best ruse is therefore to sneak out during the dead of night and complete the task well away from the prying eyes of neighbours. As morning dawns, it will enhance your reputation as a stern disciplinarian if you then send out your five-year-old, equipped with bucket and shammy, to stumble around your vehicle looking slightly confused as you bark orders regarding proper rinsing technique or remonstrations about the shoddy job he has done on the hubcaps.

Of course, with a modicum of cash to spare, it is possible to delegate the duties of car washing to the professionals:

The owner-driver need no longer walk round his car with a bucket and sponge while his hands and feet gradually become numbed by the icy water. The inventor has supplied garages with a four-legged instrument which will clean a car far more efficiently and quickly than any chauffeur. At one end is

131

Fig. 4 Jet spraying – the modern-day alternative to engaging the services of a boy scout or filthy street urchin.

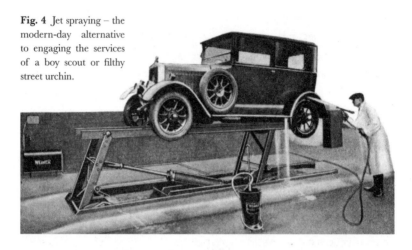

an electric motor supplying power to a high-pressure jet, which is controlled at its piston-like nozzle by a trigger [**Fig. 4**]. *Water is forced through the armoured hose at a pressure of 300 pounds to the square inch, issuing at the operator's choice either as a fine mist or as a jet which sweeps all mud and oil before it. With this instrument a car can be leathered and dried in 40 minutes instead of 3 hours.*

Professor Archibald M. Low,
The Wonder Book of Inventions, 1930

With three hours thus saved, the gentleman car owner can grab some urgently needed shut-eye or attend an emergency wine-tasting engagement at his club.

Preservation of coachwork can also be accomplished by arranging suitable board and lodgings for your vehicle. In the early days of motoring, ownership of a car was so prohibitively expensive that a vehicle was treated by its owner with the sort of reverence that might be reserved for a prize Arabian racing mare, but, sadly, these days its status has been reduced to that of a cross between a New Forest pony and a pantomime horse. Out in all weathers, left to its own devices at the roadside and given no serious consideration, the modern car makes a forlorn and untidy spectacle on our city streets. It is far better to protect one's investment by building a garage. Of course, finding adequate space for such a construction is liable to cause a few problems, but with a little imagination and some soothing words to the head gardener it is generally possible to find a small patch of fallow land somewhere between the knot garden and the temperate greenhouse that can be utilised for the scheme. The structure should be of a pleasing design: neoclassical often

Fig. 5

works well, but 'Gothic folly' or 'Thai rice barn' are not without their own appeal. For those who find that the majority of their land has been sold off due to their father's addiction to roulette and pretty ladies, the solution in **Fig. 5** might appeal. Especially suited to an urban setting, the multistorey garage can be fitted onto a plot of land no bigger than that occupied by the average two-car garage and can reap dividends from neighbours keen to rent the excess parking space.

Other maintenance responsibilities of the car owner include invigorating rituals such as filling up the fuel tank with petrol, replenishing the various types of water that are rumoured to reside in battery and radiator, and ensuring that all of the tyres are puffed up to a preordained pressure.

Fig. 6

Filling up with air, water or petrol was an awkward job in the early days of motoring. The petrol tank was usually in some un-get-atable place and a great deal of precious fuel was spilt. Today the petrol pump fills up your tank while you remain seated in the car and the only drawback is that the motorist has to stop smoking.

Professor Archibald M. Low,
The Wonder Book of Inventions, 1930

With this advice ringing in one's ears and one's pipe tobacco safely extinguished, all three of these topping-up chores may be accomplished by visiting one's local petrol station. These days petrol stations are quite hideous affairs, but there was once a time when all roadside petroleum emporia looked a bit like this (**Fig. 6**). Regrettably straw is very rarely, if ever, employed in the construction of modern-day petrol stations and in all probability the more traditionalist gentleman will find most contemporary outlets unnecessarily brutish and modern. Neon, 'Day-Glo' plastics and metal will abound and as the genteel driver reluctantly approaches and is witheringly rebuffed by the truculent gum-chewing waif in the service kiosk, it will suddenly dawn on him that (unlike the agreeable experience outlined by Professor Low) at a so-called 'self-service' outlet a driver is generally expected to serve himself. Unlike days of yore when a smiling boiler-suited attendant would happily 'fill 'er up', check the tyre pressure and water levels, and even give your windscreen a good going over, today's driver is obliged to do the petrol station's donkey work for himself. But, no matter how demeaning and wrong-headed modern practice may be, this is actually not quite as daunting as you may imagine. It is just a question of knowing in which particular orifice to insert which particular nozzle and which particular fluid to fill it with. This should be rudimentary knowledge, even for the fledgling motorist:

> *We take for granted that our novice is not ignorant of the dispositions of the car he has bought, that he has perused as much literature dealing directly with his purchase as he could conveniently come at, and that he knows, for instance, the difference between the water and petrol tanks. This is knowledge that he must possess, for no good purpose can be served by charging the wrong tank with the wrong fluid.*
>
>

The Autocar magazine, *Useful Hints and Tips for Automobilists*, 1906

No good, indeed, either to the vehicle or to one's self-esteem. Absent-mindedly topping up the petrol tank with H20, even if it is the best-quality rose water or a freshly opened bottle of San Pellegrino, is not an antic that will endear you to a carful of passengers who find themselves stranded on a dark and remote country lane or in a dangerously savage neighbourhood on the Isle of Dogs.

The final maintenance duty that the rank amateur may wish to try his hand at is the heady chore of lubrication. At first, it may appear a simple enough procedure but the layman can soon become hopelessly confused.

The advice concerning lubrication might be written in Chinese for all the help it is to the person unaccustomed to mechanical diagrams.

Richard Twelvetrees, *All About Motoring*, 1924

This is quite correct. The bewildering array of nipples, shafts and teats that need greasing may have the motor car owner questioning whether he has opened a Haynes manual or inadvertently picked up a copy of a specialist Swedish art periodical. Some engines will have helpful indications as to where lubricant should be placed, but as a general guide, it is suggested that you slap a little grease wherever a little grease seems to have hitherto resided and avoid daubing it in places occupied by petrol, water, electrical equipment or passengers.

Internal lubrication of the engine is achieved by pouring motor oil into a hole designated for the function. One of the most satisfying jobs undertaken by the gentleman motorist is testing the

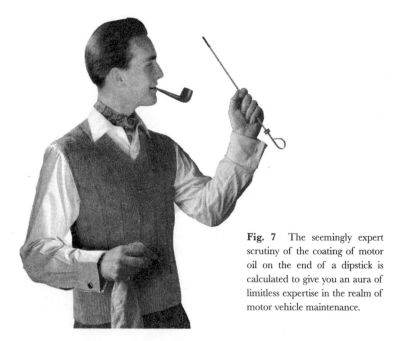

Fig. 7 The seemingly expert scrutiny of the coating of motor oil on the end of a dipstick is calculated to give you an aura of limitless expertise in the realm of motor vehicle maintenance.

level of the oil by extracting the dipstick. At moments like these he can feel preternaturally confident, pipe in mouth and oily rag in hand. He should scrutinise the black stain at the end of the stick, tut-tutting knowledgeably and inhaling tobacco smoke as a potent symbol of cogitation (**Fig. 7**). A few glugs of an oilcan later and neighbours and passengers alike will have him down as a man who 'knows his stuff...' but, of course, if truth be told, a gentleman very rarely has any intention of knowing his stuff, or, indeed, any more than is strictly necessary.

REPAIRS

Most gents have far better things to do with their time than to try to get to grips with the theory of car mechanics. Usually they are no more curious about the workings of the internal combustion engine than they are about the frightening complexities of the female reproductive system.

> *From a purely practical point of view, it is very doubtful if the average motorist of today wants to worry himself about theories at all, any more than the owner of a watch concerns himself about the internal mechanism of his timepiece.*
>
> Richard Twelvetrees, *All About Motoring*, 1924

This is all very true, but a chap who exhibits scant regard for tinkering with engines may start to question his indifference when he attempts to take to the road. Despite recent advances in car design, it is disappointing that motor manufacturers have been unable to iron out certain elements of spite and bloody-mindedness that seem inbuilt into an engine's psychological make-up:

> *On occasion one goes to start up the car and finds her more contrarily dispositioned to perform her righteous and appointed work than any – well, any other 'she's' contrariness! The car's conduct may appear equally*

unreasonable. It may be that the day before she was running perfectly, and yet now it is found that she absolutely refuses to start. Well, it is no use courting an apoplectic fit by continuing to grind the starting handle round and round.

The Motor magazine, *How to Drive a Motorcar*, 1920

Like a beached whale, a recalcitrant elephant or a dowager duchess after one too many pink gins, it is surprising how swiftly the motor car can transmogrify from a thing of majesty when in motion into a tragic lump of inert matter when deprived of forward velocity. A breakdown is likely to occur not only when you are least expecting it but also when circumstances dictate that it is the very worst possible moment for it to happen. This may be whilst rushing your wife to the county hospital to give delivery to your firstborn or, more gallingly, whilst racing down to the turf accountant to put 50 quid on a 'dead cert' in the 3.30 at Uttoxeter.

For the bachelor, breakdowns are usually calculated to happen when one is attempting to win the heart of a delightful young lady of impeccable breeding (**Fig. 8**). There you are, purring along at a fair old lick one moment, and the next ominously sputtering to a standstill. At

Fig. 8 Warm words and shared carcinogens are nothing to a lady unless accompanied by at least a feigned attempt at competence under the bonnet.

this point, your heart, so recently tap-dancing from moonbeam to moonbeam, hurtles back to earth like a malfunctioning sputnik. There is simply no point confusing your lady-love by telling her the truth and admitting that you have run out of petrol. Nine times out of ten this will undoubtedly be the case, but women are apt to lose respect for a man who appears dithering, impractical or incompetent. Motoring author Charles Baudry de Saunier knows this only too well and takes an even more extreme point of view:

> *The man who is unable to knock in a nail straight, who smashes his left thumb when he holds a hammer in his right hand, who cannot remove a screw without damaging the wood in which it is held, the man who does not know by instinct how to utilise household tools will never make a good driver.*
>
> Charles Baudry de Saunier, *The Art of Motor Driving*, 1909

Well, there we will have to differ, but it is true to say that as a gent, unaccustomed to getting his hands dirty, slowly makes his way furtively to the prow of his vehicle, opens the bonnet and peers inside, he will comprehend for the first time what it is to be truly alone. Whether your sudden stoppage happens to be caused by fuel deficiency or one of a myriad other causations is immaterial at this point. Your face, with its purposeful chin, chiselled nose and sensitive temples, desperately needs to be saved.

Even if you haven't the foggiest notion why your chariot simply refuses to budge, it is important that you now make a decent show of feigning expertise in such matters. Instruct your lady-love to remain in the vehicle and, as you walk forth, make a few authoritative pronouncements peppered with impressive buzzwords, such as: 'That damnable carburettor throttle spindle will be the death of me' or 'To hell with Smedley! I warned him that the gudgeon pin was about to give.' When safely hidden from view, this should be accompanied by exasperated huffings and realistic clanking noises made on the engine block with your briar. After around 20 minutes of this sort of carry-on it is time to re-emerge from the cover of the bonnet, but before you do, make sure you rub a small amount of engine filth across your brow, slightly tousle your hair, remove your jacket and roll up your sleeves (**Fig. 9**). Return to the driving seat, wiping your hands on a cloth and nurturing a brooding air that would make Mr Marlon Brando's performance in *Apocalypse Now* look the very essence of happy-go-lucky. Only allow the gathering storm to linger but a minute before you instantly become bright and gay. Smile broadly and admit that 'It's even got me stumped this time, darling.' With this, it is time to do what you should have done in the first place and flag down a passing combine harvester or better still a hay lorry in which you and your sweetheart can recline amongst the bales as you are transported on a romantic journey to the local village.

Tragically, there may be times when it is completely impossible to hoodwink fellow passengers, either because the radiator has run

a. WRONG   **b. RIGHT**

Fig. 9 Illustrating the crucial difference between (**a**) open ineptitude and (**b**) a feigned competency at dickering about with the internal combustion engine.

Fig. 10 In an ideal world all roadside rescue service operatives would look like this.

dry and the entire bonnet is enveloped in a steam pea-souper, or Audrey has very cleverly spotted the telltale fuel gauge, or even more disconcertingly, Gerald knows a thing or two about engines and he's pretty confident that you know next to zilch. On occasions such as these, neither admit defeat nor attempt to exhibit mechanical dexterity, but after a brief preliminary investigation merely return guffawing heartily and announce: 'What a stinker! That blighter Bingham has only gone and syphoned off all my ruddy petrol again.' This phrase is particularly useful as it can be paraphrased for almost any eventuality whether it be a dry radiator or a flat tyre.

Of course, if it does turn out to be a flat tyre, it may be necessary to invent an old sporting injury that absolutely precludes you, under strict medical advice, from any form of unpleasant bending. At this juncture, it is high time to phone one of the esteemed automobile associations to send out an emergency patrol vehicle (**Fig. 10**). Naturally, as a gentleman, you won't carry a mobile phone, but it is almost certain that someone in your entourage will have weakened and fallen prey to such an instrument. In the short time it takes to enjoy a pleasant picnic at the roadside, the cavalry are sure to have arrived. These days it can't be guaranteed that they will be as satisfyingly liveried as we see in **Fig. 10**, but this slippage in sartorial standards can possibly be overlooked as long as the patrolman in question can be cajoled into giving a half-decent salute and has the requisite know-how to get you rapidly relocated from the dusty roadside to the snug bar at the Saracen's Head public house in time for luncheon.

For those readers who actually enjoy deciphering the abstruse hieroglyphics of repair manuals, **Fig. 11** is an exploded schematic that summarises the preferred technique a gentleman should utilise in the repair of virtually any malfunction of his engine.

Fig. 11 Simple Steps for Maintenance and Repair of the Internal Combustion Engine The diagram shows the preferred method for the gentleman to while away the afternoon whilst his car is being repaired by the 'little man in the village', or a patrolman from one of the esteemed automobile associations.

1. Copy of *Racing Post.* **2.** Briar. **3.** Handlebar moustache. **4.** Brilliantined coiffure. **5.** Tweed suit. **6.** Button-back leather armchair. **7.** Armrest for maximum comfort. **8, 9 & 10.** Ergonomically proportioned carved legs for ideal sitting position. **11.** Brogues. **12, 13 & 14.** Beautifully crafted side table. **15.** Brandy glass. **16.** Bottle of Croizet 1970 vintage cognac

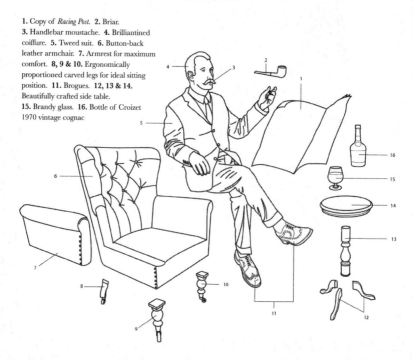

CHAPTER EIGHT

ACCESSORIES AND IMPROVEMENTS

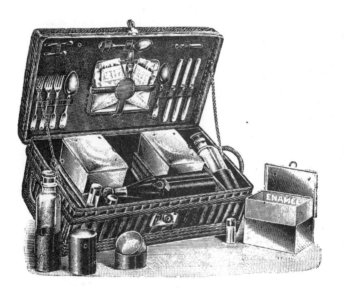

AN HISTORICAL PERSPECTIVE

These days we have become accustomed to the fact that when we purchase a new vehicle it will arrive from the manufacturer equipped with a whole range of accessories that come fitted as standard, but it was not always this way. In the early days of the automobile, the aspiring motorist who eagerly slapped his cash down on the showroom counter could expect to receive little more than the bare bones of a vehicle in return for his investment (**Fig. 1**). An engine, a chassis, the briefest smattering of coachwork and a wheel at each corner was pretty much all that could be hoped for. Similar to buying a budget airline ticket in this day and age, after finding the initial price oddly enticing, one would soon grow weak at the knees as all the hidden surcharges were gradually poured on as if from a great ladle:

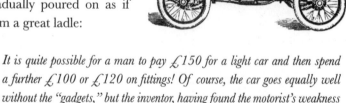

Fig. 1

It is quite possible for a man to pay £150 for a light car and then spend a further £100 or £120 on fittings! Of course, the car goes equally well without the "gadgets," but the inventor, having found the motorist's weakness for comfort and simplicity, has produced an array of tempting extras.

Professor Archibald M. Low,
The Wonder Book of Inventions, 1930

Extrapolating to account for inflation, £120 in today's money is roughly equivalent to the cost of a four-week luxury Caribbean cruise, or if you don't wish to curtail your holiday plans, around about half the price you could expect to raise if you sold one of your kidneys on the illicit transplant market (which, come to think of it, would happily cover the cost of both the extras and the cruise).

Fig. 2

Amongst the 'extras' that the driver-owner was expected to purchase were dashboard basics that the modern motorist now takes totally for granted.

*There is no end to the number of fittings which the enthusiast may have upon his dashboard – most of them very costly and of doubtful utility. But a good carriage clock [**Fig. 2**] is a necessity, while a gradiometer, for measuring the gradients over which the car is travelling, is a rather interesting accessory to a touring car. There are 'speedometers' now made which I believe are very accurate and trustworthy in recording in miles per hour the rate at which the car is travelling; but I doubt whether they give much pleasure to the average owner of a car.*

A.B. Filson Young, *The Complete Motorist*, 1904

As insight into the human psyche goes, Mr Filson Young does not acquit himself well here. These days, knowing precisely at what velocity one is travelling gives a great deal of pleasure to a great many car owners and especially to those of the aforementioned Clarksonite Tendency.

Other optional add-ons that lent a touch of luxury to a car included headlamps and motor horns. Today these are gadgets that no self-respecting driver would consider doing without and it seems extraordinary that they could ever have been regarded as discretionary. As we have seen in Chapter Five, a motor horn is the chief method by which the motorist communicates with fellow road users, either to encourage, cajole, warn, thank or, more often than not, punish. The driver who decides of his own free will that the motor horn can be cast aside as an unwarranted frippery must be a very odd cove indeed – either limply pacifist or extraordinarily self-effacing. By 1900 two types of horn were available, the reassuringly brassy hand-tweaked hooter (**Fig. 3a**) and the new fangled foot-pumped variety (**Fig. 3b**). It would be another decade yet before the efficiently strident electric horn would make chastising errant drivers and harrying pedestrians far more rewarding and enjoyable.

Headlights were similarly regarded as useful but non-essential accoutrements, affording the motorist the luxury of being able to drive his vehicle at night without having to resort to the exigencies of street lights, extrasensory perception or excessive carrot consumption. If headlamps were purchased then the motorist was advised to acquire items which would at least be adequate to the task:

If one happens to be driving with only small headlamps, then it is preferable to slow down very considerably, as the risk of running into anything at the side of the road is considerably enhanced.

The Motor magazine, *How to Drive a Motorcar*, 1914

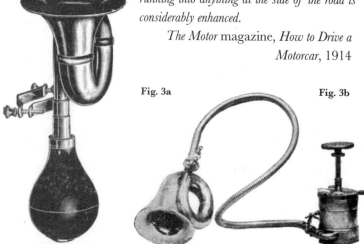

Fig. 3a   **Fig. 3b**

Indeed, it soon became apparent that a good strong pair of headlamps might be a very sensible addition to every car, as regularly colliding with farmyard animals or turfing the local vicar off his bicycle after the hours of nightfall wasn't likely to do them, your reputation or your paintwork any good whatsoever. After experimenting with lamps fuelled by oil (**Fig. 4**) or acetylene, the electric headlight was finally invented in 1898, making night motoring a safer and more pleasant experience for driver, livestock and clergy alike.

Fig. 4

Perhaps one of the greatest gifts the inventor has made to the motorist is electric lighting. I can remember the days when night driving was an ordeal and only the direst necessity took the motorist out after dark.

Professor Archibald M. Low,
The Wonder Book of Inventions, 1930

Other innovations, which seem to have been tailor-made for the gentleman motorist, were designed to solve the tricky business of lighting up a pipe or cigarette whilst remaining firmly in control of one's vehicle. The former of these problems is yet to be solved as igniting one's pipe is essentially a dual-handed affair involving sustained lung to flame co-ordination, but the tricky business of firing up a gasper whilst behind the wheel seems to have been resolved satisfactorily:

[There] is a cigarette-lighter, which not only lights up for him, but, by the suction action of the engine, takes the first puff for him, so that he need not take his hands from the wheel! A more recent electrical type hands a lighted cigarette to the driver, who has merely to pull a knob.

Professor Archibald M. Low,
The Wonder Book of Inventions, 1930

It is curious that in these so-called advanced times cigarette lighters of the 'first puff' and 'knob pulling' variety no longer seem to exist. It is only to be hoped that this book may draw the attention of manufacturers towards this obvious and lamentable gap in the market.

A further outstanding car accessory that seems to have fallen out of favour in modern times is the radiator mascot. There was a time when no self-respecting car owner would deign to view the road ahead of him without a small figurine of a naked lady or a rampant beast cluttering up his field of vision. Unfortunately, the design of modern cars isn't very accommodating to the driver who wishes to upgrade his vehicle in this fashion. Even if you did manage to Araldite a Lalique eagle's head to the front of your Vauxhall Astra, it is very doubtful in these larcenous times that it would still be there by the time you set off the next morning. Radiator mascots were not only objects of outstanding beauty, they could serve practical functions too:

> *Another fascinating and useful invention which can be fitted to cars is a miniature lighthouse which stands on the radiator cap, combining a thermometer with a tell-tale lamp of any colour. Here the hot water of the cooling system acts directly on the mercury, warning the driver of the point at which his engine is likely to become inefficient through overheating, while the bulb burns only so long as his rear light is working.*

> Professor Archibald M. Low,
> *The Wonder Book of Inventions*, 1930

MODERN ACCESSORIES

Even though the modern car arrives in a state of completion that frees the new owner from having to immediately stump up extra cash to render it halfway roadworthy, he will still find that there is a jolly array of gift items that he can purchase for his vehicle.

With reference to the previous chapter, the first accessory that a gent should set about purchasing for his new motor car is a fully equipped toolkit. As we have seen, it is very unlikely that he will have either the requisite skills or inclination ever to use such an item, but neglecting to purchase a toolkit would be tantamount to admitting that he is a rank amateur of the highway. Extraordinarily pleasurable afternoons can be spent comparing and contrasting the various tools it contains with other motorists you meet, most of whom will be equally clueless as to their utilisation as you are yourself (**Fig. 5**). This is not to conclude that a toolkit is of no practical value; indeed it may be, insomuch as it is available for use by any competent passenger or pedestrian who is close at hand in the event of an emergency. **Fig. 6** (overleaf) illustrates the anatomy of a well thought-out toolkit.

When exhibiting one's impressive panoply of repair instruments to fellow motorists, it is important to have a working knowledge of their names and one or two tales to relate in connection with their

Fig. 5 An effusive gent feigns expertise regarding his newly acquired electric car jack. Meanwhile, a fellow gentleman motorist nonchalantly formulates the most proficient next move to 'out-gadget' his adversary.

GENTLEMEN'S OAK TOOL CHEST

Fig. 6 The Contents of a Gentleman's Toolkit
Upper layers should contain a full array of masculine ironmongery including various sizes of 'Auto Cle' spanner, mole grips and a motor jack. These conceal a far more practical final layer containing corkscrew, hip flask, playing cards, grooming accoutrements, spare briars and a trusty Webley for taking potshots at game birds and repelling mobs of feral youths.

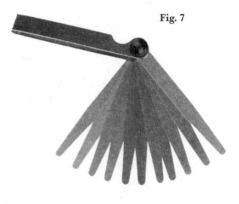

Fig. 7

usage. Make reference to less common tools such as the gland nut wrench, mole grip or nipple spanner, or concoct some exotic guff about the feeler gauge (**Fig. 7**). In reality, the latter will only ever have been extracted from its box for the purposes of wafting about a bit, but don't let that stop your imagination from soaring: 'Don't know what I would have done in India in '97 without my trusty feeler gauge. Adjusted the spark plugs with it in Delhi, used it to spread my Gentleman's Relish whilst on a lunchtime picnic outside Shahpura and in the evening, in Jaipur, lent it to the Maharani of Jaisalmer as a makeshift fan.' This fanciful outpouring is designed to dazzle your audience with so much scintillating information that it will hopefully deflect any possibility of serious technical talk. Your fellow motorist will of course attempt to counter your feigned knowledge by lobbing a few one-upmanship gambits of his own and thus a full afternoon of satisfying tool banter lies ahead.

Another addition to a car which no right-minded driver should be without is a wicker hamper designed along the lines of the Motor Tea Basket illustrated in **Fig. 8** (overleaf). Early genteel motorists realised that unless they were to be at the culinary mercy of gnarled peasantry in roadside coaching inns it was essential to ensure that a fully stocked hamper accompanied them wherever they went.

A picnic basket should always be carried. This saves much time. It is delightful to stop at some charming spot and lunch, or have tea in the open air. For years I was bothered by the unsolved difficulty of keeping the butter cool. At last I overcame it by having a vulcanized cardboard case made, and

Fig. 8 **MOTOR TEA BASKET FOR FOUR PERSONS.**

Size, 22 by 12½ by 7½ in.   Electro-plated fittings.

Best quality Basket, lined leather throughout.

Contents :—Stove lamp and extra spirit container, kettle fitted with screw lid and cap to spout, tea infuser, 1 provision box enamel lined, 1 large provision box enamel lined, 1 tea and sugar box, 4 enamel cups, saucers and plates, 4 ivory handle knives, 4 electro-plated tea spoons, 1 milk bottle, 1 butter pot, enamel lining, 1 match box.

Price complete... £5 17 6

Above fittings in the new patent (No. 29,305) dust proof
    case, covered green pegamoid 7 12 6

fixed by straps and staples on the step... My basket is not 'fitted'. Everything is made of aluminium, spoons, forks, tea-caddy and sugar box, plates and large sandwich case. I take many of those delightful pressed cardboard plates, with extra grease-proof linings which can be thrown away and save much washing up.

The Baroness Campbell Von Laurentz,
My Motor Milestones, 1913

These days of course the entire road network is set up with the refreshment of the driver in mind. Service areas on motorways and Americanised roadside eateries now make the packing of a picnic basket full to the brim with appetising morsels even more essential.

The list of gizmos designed to assist the motorist and make his life more comfortable is almost endless. The gent wishing to satisfy his curiosity may be tempted to visit a modern car accessory shop, but it is extremely doubtful that he will find much on its shelves that will coincide with his gentlemanly tastes. Cradles for mobile phones, satellite navigation systems, Bluetooth hands-free sets (whatever those might be), in-car stereo systems, kits for this, kits for that – such things might be fine and dandy for the Xbox generation, but they are guaranteed to curdle a gentleman's soul and put his feet on a one-way trajectory towards the exit.

Before he departs, however, there is possibly one item he may wish to consider purchasing. As a man of rarefied tastes, he will surely have hitherto poured scorn on the customised adhesive windscreen visors often seen adorning Ford Cortinas and other such vehicles, dismissing them as irredeemably vulgar, but one should never be too hasty to judge. Vulgarity has more to do with context and sentiment than intrinsic worth. In the right hands, the sun visor can be used to convey a range of radical, poetic or inspirational messages that will not only cement your credentials as an aesthete of the asphalt, but will also be educational and improving to others. **Fig. 9a** (overleaf) illustrates the traditional bland utilisation of the visor, whereas **Figs. 9b to 9d** demonstrate a far more enlightened approach to their usage.

Another practice which may initially repel the gent is the great cluster of tawdry ornamentation that many motorists insist on suspending from their rear-view mirrors. Classically these will consist of dreadful bits of tat such as fuzzy dice, beads, luminous plastic St Christopher medals and air fresheners shaped like small trees which unaccountably make the car smell of a foetid urinal disguised as a pine forest. All four should be avoided, but this is not to say that each and every item that dangles from the ceiling of a car is naturally infra dig. In their stead, try adorning your mirror with choice items from your ethnographic collection. This might be a highly decorated penis gourd from New Guinea, a necklace of wampum or an amusing shrunken

Figs. 9a–9d Guidance for car visor messages. The unimaginative usage of the sun visor in (**a**) should be rejected in favour of more inspirational aphorisms and mantras. George Melly's quotation (**b**) invites fellow motorists to emulate your bold individualism, whereas Oscar Wilde's (**c**) promotes gentlemanly self-knowledge. A slightly more outré tone may be struck by employing Aleister Crowley's occultist adage (**d**) in the hope of drawing attention to the arbitrary nature of road traffic laws.

head. These items will add flair to your vehicle's interior and can also act as an ice breaker when giving a lift to people you don't know very well, such as hitchhikers, work colleagues or the headmistress of the new school at which you have just enrolled your children.

A further example of how well worn clichés of car decoration can be reinvented for the gentleman motorist lies in the back window shelf area. Normally this is a rather squalid region of a car, one that usually serves as a repository for boxes of man-sized tissues, half-eaten sandwiches, dead pets and so on, but those who notice its existence will see it as a venue for self-expression. Let's not humiliate ourselves with 'Baby On Board' signage or wackily designed sun shades, but instead concentrate on its staple occupant – the nodding dog. Overdue for a rehaul, especially after a series of increasingly irritating television commercials, the knowing art lover might be moved to commission a local craftsman, especially if he lives close to Carrara or the alabaster workshops of Florence, to put a lovingly realised, greyhound-sized nodding sphinx in its place (**Fig. 10**). A sculpture of these proportions is not strictly sensible in terms of rear-view mirror visibility, but real Art can never be expected to be safe.

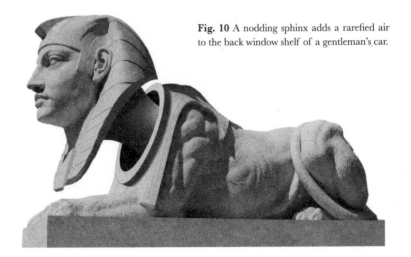

Fig. 10 A nodding sphinx adds a rarefied air to the back window shelf of a gentleman's car.

IMPROVEMENTS AND CUSTOMISATION

If you are blessed with ownership of a 1954 Bentley Continental sports saloon by H. J. Mulliner & Co. of Chiswick, it is unlikely you will have given much thought to customisation. Trying to improve on such a vehicle, with its exquisitely modelled coachwork and understated *marqueterie* interior, would be, like a politician's smile, an empty and grotesque gesture. But for the rest of us, who possibly have to make do with more modest makes of car, customisation is a splendid way for a gent of limited means to own a thoroughly stylish vehicle.

By acquiring some of the accessories in the previous section, the gentleman driver will have already gone some way to adapting his vehicle to his rarefied needs. The line between the acquisition of accessories and a full-blown customising of a vehicle is necessarily a rather blurred one, but generally speaking the difference is governed by the degree of hacksawing, hammering, welding, tinkering and gluing that is involved. Some fellows become so excitable at the very idea of individualising their cars that they will immediately go out and join a night class on the subject, happily donning a welding mask and wielding an acetylene torch in furtherance of their goals. But it goes without saying that most gentlemen who are seized by a craving for an 'upgrade' will probably get someone else to do the donkey work for them. A thorough revamping of a vehicle, however undertaken, can still be extremely rewarding.

The customising of vehicles is said to be a particular preoccupation in the United States of America, where there seems to be no limit to the excesses that car owners are prepared to go to in order to 'pimp their ride'. These include idiosyncrasies such as under-car lighting (presumably for the admirable purpose of assisting the elderly in the retrieval of dropped keys) and ruses to pep up the suspension of a car so that its front wheels bounce alarmingly. Perhaps this too is designed to help the elderly dislodge trapped fish bones and other built-up nutrients from their jaded tracheae.

Even if we are not as steeped in concern for our senior citizenry as our transatlantic cousins, there is a growing trend on this side of the pond for a gentleman to personalise his 'ride' into a vehicle more suited as a venue for self-expression and contemplation. For the flamboyantly minded gent, for whom the simple lines of Mr Issigonis's classic Morris Minor are not enough, there is a great deal of modification that can be made. Seeking guidance on how to proceed, perhaps we could refer to *The Motor* magazine's *How to Drive a Motorcar of 1914*: '*The capable driver usually has the appearance of being as much at home at the seat of the car which he is driving as one would expect to find him when comfortably ensconced in an armchair by his own fireside.*' In **Fig. 11** we see the work of an enthusiast who has taken this advice quite literally and, using a salvaged marble fireplace, has converted his dashboard into an approximation of a Regency drawing room. The effect is completed by the addition of an LCD screen below the speedometer depicting the flickering flames of an open hearth. Purists might baulk at the use of a fake fire, but real flames quite so close to the engine cannot be recommended and

Fig. 11

a chimney does tend to disfigure the bonnet, as well as obscuring the driver's line of vision.

Another vehicle (**Fig. 12**) has been converted into a kitsch Gothic love nest, no doubt for use by a predatory roué. A sumptuous Chesterfield bench replaces both front seats and the upholstery is augmented by the addition of stained glass windows, corbels, ocelot-skin door panels and a Murano glass chandelier.

For further guidance on the customisation of the car's exterior, the reader should study the following pages. These illustrate several different approaches to the art of converting mundane and modest vehicles into chariots far more suited to the needs of a gentleman – a concept known as 'primping one's ride'.

Fig. 12

AHOY CHUM! PRIMP MY RIDE

The Bubble Royce

This converted Isetta retains maximum parking convenience as well as its two-cylinder, two-stroke motorcycle engine, allowing the driver all the manoeuvrability and economy of the bubble car, but 'primped' to give it the nobility and hauteur of a vintage Rolls. Especially convenient for those nights out in town, enabling the driver to cock a snook at traffic wardens by being able to squeeze into the snuggest of spaces when visiting Covent Garden Opera House.

The Gondola Reliant Robin

Comedy vehicles such as the Reliant Robin are not first on anyone's list of romantic transport options, but by affixing the prow of a gondola to its bonnet, the owner of this van conjures up images of the Canale Grande and the Ponte di Rialto, effectively hoodwinking passengers into believing that the grubby old fibreglass crate they are hurtling along in is actually the veritable bee's knees of exotic sophistication.

The Block Print Cortina

It is possible to liven up an extraordinarily dull vehicle such as this Cortina by papering it with a high-quality block-printed wallpaper, preferably modelled on the one you saw on the walls of the music room during a weekend stay as the guest of the 8th Earl of Stapleforth. Effectively converting your car into an inverse drawing room renders it highly conducive to reciting memorised chunks of Wildean wit or listening to the songs of Noël Coward on a car stereo system (potted aspidistra as extra).

The Ben Hur

Based on the chariot scene in the popular Hollywood film of the same name, the Ben Hur is a simple conversion job that entails the addition of razor-sharp sabre blades to your hubcaps. With these in place the traditionally 'cuddly' Morris Minor becomes an impressively cinematic but brutally vicious war chariot that is capable of inspiring unprecedented levels of respect in the minds of jeering yobbos, persistent traffic wardens or sluggish pedestrians.

The Sinclair 'C' Phaeton

The plastic idiocy known as the Sinclair C5 was unsurprisingly a commercial flop when it was launched in 1985. Its failure was due in no small part to its diminutive proportions, which made it almost invisible to fellow road users, subjecting the driver to the continuous danger of being puréed by heavy goods vehicles into human chutney. Perhaps it is now time to dust off that model you've had sitting in the garden shed all these years and give it the grandeur and visibility it always lacked by harnessing it up to a trio of thoroughbreds.

The Pick-Up Divan

Turning up to an amorous tryst in a workaday vehicle such as the pick-up truck or open-backed van is very unlikely to butter the parsnips of any young debutante of quality. Converting your vehicle into a four-poster fantasia may not be the most subtle approach to wooing but hopefully a prospective lover will be so bowled over by opulence, brocade and soft furnishings that she will fail to notice that the term 'pick-up' is imbued with decidedly lubricious connotations.

The Thatchback

The Morris Traveller's half-timbered frame naturally invites a logical route to its customisation. Employing a master thatcher to convert the roof of your vehicle into that of a picturesque farmhouse will mean that even if you dwell amidst the urban sprawl, you may still experience the rustic charms of Merry Olde England without the inconvenience of ever having to set foot in the countryside.

The Parthenon Transit

A reconstruction from the Greek original, the pleasing classical lines of the Parthenon lend a much-needed touch of style and class to this all-too-vulgar commercial vehicle. The transit van is renowned as being the transport option of choice for those dealing in artifacts of dubious legitimacy. In the light of this, it can only be assumed that the 7th Earl of Elgin would have wholeheartedly approved of this fitting and elegant tribute.

CHAPTER NINE

RECREATIONAL DRIVING

GETTING AWAY FROM IT ALL

O nce the motorist has experienced the joys and excitements of driving around his own locale, he will undoubtedly start to grow curious as to the possibilities of travelling further afield purely for the pleasure it affords. Even from the earliest days of the automobile it became apparent that ownership of a vehicle bestowed a new-found freedom to travel hither and yon in the pursuit of recreation. Especially after the development of affordable mass-produced cars, post-World War I, 'getting away from it all' became a bit of an obsession. From now on there was nothing other than the shackles of employment and lack of cash to prevent a gent from *going a-gypsying*, seeing more of his own country and even possibly venturing to those territories that come under the slightly alarming umbrella of 'abroad'.

MOTORWAY AND LONG-DISTANCE DRIVING

These days, most pleasure trips and domestic holidays commence with unappealing stints on our motorway network, but prior to 1958 such vast roads simply didn't exist and the growing popularity of the motor car in the 1920s was beginning to prove something of a problem on roads that had essentially been designed with horse-drawn vehicles in mind:

> *The roads within a fifty mile radius of London, are, on a fine Saturday or Sunday, without exaggeration a motor pandemonium. One day last summer, it was my extraordinary ill-luck to drive up from Brighton to London in the evening between 6 o'clock and 9 o'clock, and as a result of those three*

164

appalling hours, I decided but "life and death" shall drag me, either in my own or someone else's car to Brighton during the summer.
John Prioleau, *Motoring for Women*, 1925

Those of a nostalgic hue will be pleased to hear that these days, despite huge expansion of the road network, a corresponding exponential increase in car ownership means that very little has changed. As soon as a large proportion of the population gets it into its head to get away from it all ('it all' being the people, congestion and exhaust fumes of town or city) then they merely end up taking it all with them, translocating the hideousness of their lives a few miles up the road in vast static islands of vehicles, perhaps occupying the entirety of the M25 or forming a 15-mile tailback on the M1.

This is why a gentleman only rarely deigns to travel by motorway. At times he might try to fool himself that the motorway network has a brutalist integrity. He may even be heard vehemently arguing his corner at dinner parties, maintaining that the Westway, or A40(M) (**Fig. 1**) is one of the most thrillingly avant-garde sculptural pieces of the 20th century, or that, photographed from space, Spaghetti Junction is more beautiful than the intricacies of design adorning the ceilings of the Hall of the Abencerrajes at the Alhambra, but in his heart of hearts he very much doubts if this is true.

Fig. 1 London's Westway – thrillingly avant-garde art statement or lumpish concrete monstrosity?

The gentleman's chief objection to motorways is their utter tedium. Being bereft of charming little tea rooms, coaching inns and viewing spots from which to dash off a watercolour or two, they result in being not only mind-numbingly dull, but also actively harmful, as travelling along them for prolonged periods is known to cause a variety of medical conditions such as aching limbs, cramp, tetchiness, deep vein thrombosis, absent-minded nose picking and stress-related tuneless whistling. In the past, the solution to long-distance driving fatigue was relatively simple:

> *In long-distance driving a rest by the wayside for a few minutes is often time well spent. Otherwise, changing the attitude, by holding the steering wheel in different positions will afford some relief.* [**Fig. 2**]
>
> How to Drive a Light Car or a Cyclecar, by the staff of
> The Light Car and Cyclecar, 1917

Sadly, nowadays such a 'rest by the wayside' is only possible if one is willing to subject oneself to the indignity of visiting a 'motorway services'. These are modern *caravanserais* placed at strategic distances throughout the motorway network, but unlike the original Turkish wayside inns of old, the gent should not expect much by way of picturesque scenes involving camels and fountains, but in their stead some tawdry unattractive bunker a-throng with tawdry unattractive customers. To visit such places one needs to be very desperate – very desperate for nutrition, very desperate for fuel, very desperate because your car is falling apart or very desperate to perform a bodily function. No one, other than those with a pronounced sense of irony or an MA in the Construction and Design of 1960s Road Infrastructure could possibly dream of visiting a motorway services for any other reason.

On driving along the slip road to a motorway services, you will first notice that some cursory attempts at landscaping have been made. Scrubby bushes, grassy knolls and depressed-looking saplings – hardly 'Capability' Brown, but still, other than the 'exit' sign, this is going to be the most favourable aspect you are likely to encounter. Enjoy it while it lasts. It all rapidly goes downhill from here.

Parking your 1938 Bugatti 57SC Atlantic as unassumingly as is possible, enter the main building, which you may be forgiven at first glance for mistaking for a furniture warehouse or crematorium. The 'foyer' will be furnished with various tawdry kiosks and populated with the sort of people you do not usually mix with. Do not lose your nerve. At this point, a fixed objective is required. Prepare for a strategic strike. If your needs are chiefly lavatorial in nature, then you will be happy

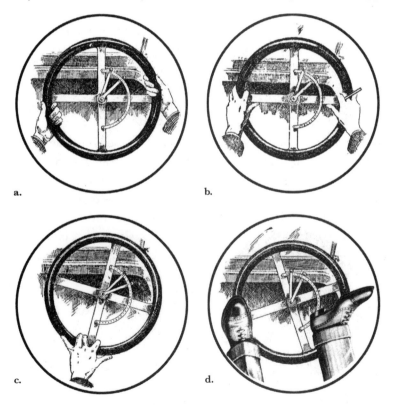

Fig. 2 The different positions at the wheel which might afford relief for the weary driver. (**a**) Standard reverse grip. (**b**) Forward grip with soothing Sobranie cocktail cigarette. (**c**) Nonchalant single-handed. (**d**) Extremely nonchalant hands-free.

to hear that these will usually be the closest facilities to hand. A brisk attitude is required. There will be no lavatory attendants dispensing fresh towels and cologne, but show courage and cope as manfully as you can.

A visit to the 'restaurant' presents a different set of problems. As shocking as it may seem, there will be no *maître d'* to greet you and guide you to your table. You will have to queue up at a 'self-service buffet' and select your own food from a series of glass cabinets. These will consist of unappetising dishes, with nary a devilled kidney, a kedgeree, a quail's egg or a *cervelles au beurre noir* in sight (but try

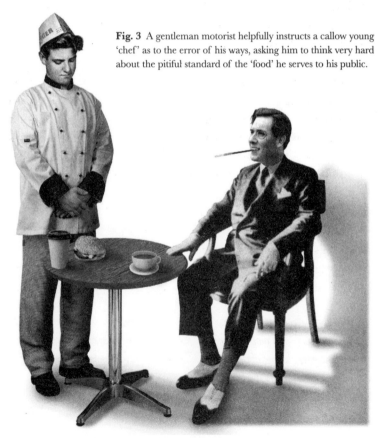

Fig. 3 A gentleman motorist helpfully instructs a callow young 'chef' as to the error of his ways, asking him to think very hard about the pitiful standard of the 'food' he serves to his public.

ordering these dishes all the same, as only the levers of demand can ever be expected to shift the vicissitudes of supply). The recommended plan is to keep things simple and order a dish that you feel that the staff of such an eatery might be capable of cooking with a passable level of competence. With this in mind, a cup of tea (sadly of an unspecified variety) and a round of buttered toast might be your best bet. The tea will probably appear as a cup of boiling water with a desultory teabag bobbing about in it. Milk and sugar will have to be sourced from a grey plastic drawer of 'portion-controlled' sachets and cartons.

After finishing lunch, it is frightfully important to summon the chef to one's table and give him an appraisal of his performance. Perhaps enquire whether the butter was locally sourced or if the wheat used to make the bread is organic. Finally, give him a short impromptu lecture on how you think he could improve upon the abhorrent muck he currently serves – only couched in slightly subtler terms (**Fig. 3**).

This important work done, it is time to speed back onto the highway and embark upon the rest of your long-distance jaunt. It is at this point in the journey, after lunch and with the winter sun setting behind the oil refinery, that the gentleman motorist will be at his most vulnerable. Thoughts of his relaxed week ahead in a small retreat in Pembrokeshire, coupled with listening to the afternoon play on Radio Four (no doubt chronicling the sexual dissatisfactions of a middle-aged middle-class housewife – as most of them do), may have his eyelids growing heavier and heavier by the second. Beware! The biggest danger of long-distance and motorway driving might just be about to strike:

Falling asleep at the wheel often causes accidents. If you are ill, do not drive. Liquor and monoxide poison are enemies of expertness. Heart disease or any other chronic ailment which might mean loss of consciousness should keep you out of the driver's seat.

Richard Alexander Douglas,
Common Sense in Driving Your Car, 1936

Indeed, even those happily unafflicted by 'chronic ailments' or acute alcoholism should be warned of the dangers of impromptu snoozing:

> *The writer has had experience of drivers falling asleep on more than one occasion, and once when on a long night journey, entirely given up to the charms of Morpheus on the back seat, suddenly woke to find himself with torn clothes and scratched face and hands, in the middle of a hedge. The explanation was that the driver, who was a thoroughly moderate man in every way, and healthier and stronger physically than ninety-nine men out of a hundred, had fallen asleep, the car had jumped the grass curb, and he awoke only in time to assist in stopping the car when its progress was mainly arrested by the hedge.*
>
> The Motor magazine, *How to Drive a Motorcar*, 1920

Once again the unforgiving terrain of the motorway is found to be lacking in this respect. There is very little likelihood of such a devil-may-care and amusing outcome if one happens to nod off whilst powering down the fast lane of a busy motorway.

PLEASURE TRIPS

The sort of recreational driving that the gent will indulge in most frequently are those journeys of no more than a few hours' duration, generally known as 'pleasure trips'. This is a bit of a misnomer because as life progresses such trips become less and less pleasurable.

As a dashing young blade the term may well be accurate, as most trips undertaken will consist of days away with chums and spirited debutantes, for picnics, days at the beach, gymkhanas, sightseeing jaunts or orgiastic Dionysian woodland parties organised by the Hellfire Club, but as a gent's responsibilities and family commitments grow, 'pleasure trips' will increasingly become more stodgy affairs. By the time he has reached his late thirties, the idealised image of a family outing depicted in **Fig. 4** will bear scant relation to the truth. So-called 'pleasure trips' will consist of ferrying moaning offspring and sour-faced aged aunts on day trips to stately homes and faded seaside resorts.

The essential element of pleasure tripping, however, is to refuse to be rushed:

> *Now when we set out on a pleasure trip, if such a thing is possible in these times, or ever was, as is the rule nowadays we are on business bent, a calm, contemplative spirit should be engendered. It is the greatest mistake to set out with the fixed intention of getting to a certain place by a definite time, if it can be possibly avoided, as it can in 9 cases out of 10. A dolce far niente spirit should inspire our motoring.*
>
> How to Drive a Light Car or a Cyclecar, by the staff of
> The Light Car and Cyclecar, 1917

Ah yes, the *sweet doing nothing* of the Italians is the only way to proceed. If anything, pleasure tripping, properly approached, should be primarily

Fig. 4

about the journey and not the destination. It should therefore take in various essentials: a few hairpin bends, some humpbacked bridges, and a winding road through heather moorland are some of the more traditional features. The slightly more adventurous pleasure tripper may wish to indulge in placing wagers with chums based on challenges such as who can scare the most clergy or produce the most amusing skid.

TOURING

The only problem with pleasure tripping around Great Britain is that just as you are getting used to driving in a certain direction for an hour or two you are likely to bump into one of its edges and be forced to turn your car around and go back from whence you came. After a while, the gentleman motorist may begin to think that motoring on his home isle is a tad limiting and start to crave a spot of *rouler sans frontières*. The best place for this, as the phrase might suggest, is abroad.

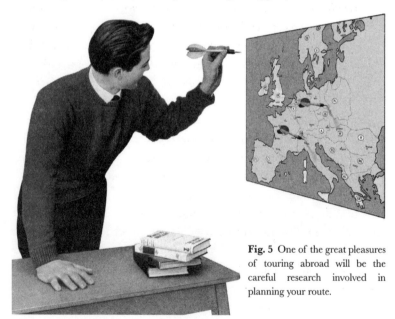

Fig. 5 One of the great pleasures of touring abroad will be the careful research involved in planning your route.

'Abroad' will strike the gentleman as a disconcerting place at first. He will doubtless be familiar with Paris, Monte Carlo, St Moritz, New York, Rome, Milan and so on. In fact, he will probably own *pieds-à-terre* in several of these cities, but the provincial regions of 'abroad' are a very different kettle of fish to their sophisticated cities and opulent resorts. One only needs to consider how much Norfolk differs from London to get the picture. The provinces of France, for example, may well turn out to be every bit as inbred and divergent from their capital, but at least in Norfolk one would be reasonably likely to find a decent cup of tea and a population who are capable of expressing themselves in an almost-comprehensible variant of the English language. No such guarantees can be made abroad.

Another factor that the motorist will have to take into account is the expense that a touring holiday may incur:

> *"Is it very expensive to take a car abroad?" is one of the first questions I am generally asked. My answer is "No, if you go the right way about it." You must of course speak French, and not stay in the large and expensive hotels. No doubt you have been told of the delightful little hotels and inns which you will meet with in France, of the charming landlords and clever chefs.*
>
> The Baroness Campbell Von Laurentz,
> *My Motor Milestones*, 1913

On reflection, this description does sound a damn sight more agreeable than anything one is ever likely to encounter in Norfolk. Perhaps 'abroad' will not turn out to be so daunting after all.

Much fun can be had in meticulously researching and scientifically planning your tour (**Fig. 5**). Even if a misspent youth spent avoiding lessons and smoking fags behind the school bicycle sheds means that one's French vocabulary amounts to only what one can scribble on the back of a packet of *Gitanes*, this should not deter one from grasping the nettle and heading off in pursuit of *kilomètre après kilomètre* of free open road.

The delights of motoring can be enjoyed nowhere so fully as in France, and it should be the ambition of everyone who has a motor-car to carry it, as soon as possible, across the Channel.

A.B. Filson Young, *The Complete Motorist*, 1904

Fig. 6

The logical place to start one's tour of 'abroad' is by crossing the Channel to Dieppe or Calais. These days one has alternatives. One can travel to Calais from Folkestone via the *Eurotunnel Le Shuttle* or of course one can still catch a ferry. Naturally, most gentlemen will err on the side of the nautical. Not only does sea travel still have a residual romance that scuttling underground like a sewer rat lacks, but a ferry crossing gives the gent an opportunity to commission a costume of a suitably maritime flavour which he can change into for the 90 or so minutes it takes to complete the crossing (**Fig. 6**). This suit of clothing will also come in useful if his final destination is expected to be Nice or some other resort on the French Riviera.

However, some advice from John Prioleau may seem to cast doubt on the value of commissioning new suits of clothes specifically for your tour:

The principal rule in laying your plans for a motoring tour is to cut down the quantity of clothes you carry to the absolute minimum.

John Prioleau, *Motoring for Women*, 1925

Before he starts rummaging around in his luggage and jettisoning items, the gent should bear in mind that this advice is chiefly directed at the lady motorist, and what constitutes the 'absolute minimum' for a lady will be a very different thing from what it constitutes for a gentleman. If anything a man must wrestle the primitive and barbaric side of his nature which urges him to travel light. The whole concept of gentlemanliness pivots on his taming such bestial behaviour and thus unleashing the inner, civilised dandy. If anything, unlike a lady, a gent should err on the side of excess in the costume department and even then he will probably tend to under-pack.

On embarking on a cross-channel ferry, you may well be disappointed to find that general standards of sartorial style are very much beneath those of your own. Shorts, baseball caps and T-shirts will abound and you may swiftly come to the conclusion that you are mixing with exactly the same breed of people that you have previously encountered when stopping at the motorway services, and unfortunately you would be completely right in this assumption. But don't let it worry you unduly. Merely push on and secure yourself a comfortable corner in which to unpack your luncheon hamper (the food on board also being on a par with a motorway services). If you have engaged staff for the journey, then whilst they lay out your picnic, it is only polite if you pop up to the bridge and introduce yourself to the captain. All etiquette thus adhered to, a tolerably comfortable crossing can be made.

Aboard ship, despite some overtly Gallic nods towards your final destination, such as announcements in French and a few suspect-looking staff, essentially you are still safely in Blighty. 'Abroad' proper starts the moment you drive off the boat. This is why you must select your touring car wisely. It must be chosen in order to gain the respect

Fig. 7

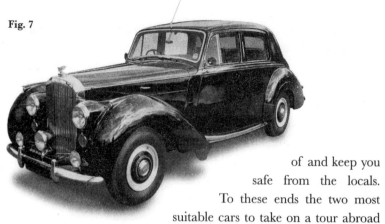

of and keep you safe from the locals. To these ends the two most suitable cars to take on a tour abroad are a 1954 Bentley Continental R-type (**Fig. 7**), so-called because it was specifically designed for high-speed touring on European roads, and a 1939 Lagonda LG45 V12 with bodywork by Frank Feeley. These are guaranteed to make their mark when arriving at any small villages abroad and with luck will have the villagers scurrying around trying to be helpful and to please you.

Once the gentleman has gained shore it will immediately strike him exactly how contrary foreigners can be. Not only will they speak a language that he barely understands but they will also attempt to unsettle him with a bloody-minded insistence on driving on the wrong side of the road. Adapting to such aberrant practices can put a strain on a gent's nerves and, fatigued, he may wish to seek out his initial overnight stay sooner rather than later. The first thing he will notice on arriving at a suitably quaint place is that they dress rather differently from himself. In fact, the further he strays from English shores the more outlandish costumes are liable to become. As a general guide, the peasantry of Europe will probably look a little like this (**Fig. 8**) or some variant on the theme. Despite their eccentricities it is important to treat them with due respect. Speak clearly and authoritatively in English and with luck they will do your bidding, but bear in mind that things you may take for granted back in Blighty will not necessarily be freely available when on the Continent:

The chief objections to these small hotels is the difficulty of procuring a bath for yourself and a hose for the car.

The Baroness Campbell Von Laurentz,
My Motor Milestones, 1913

Once he has gradually grown accustomed to the irritations caused by shortages in commodities such as water, electricity, proper beer and soap, the gentleman will begin to find the Continent is not at all as bad as he had expected. The main thing is to moderate one's pace and avoid planning an itinerary that involves breaking one's neck to travel between locations that are placed too far apart for pleasurable motoring. It is also recommended that the driving duties are shared out amongst one's chums so that none of the party gets overly tired:

On August 25th 1901, we started on our tour, our party consisted of my husband and myself and our small motor boy, B., the fourth seat being occupied by our luggage... Now, for the only time during the tour, my arm got a little tired and stiff, and I let B. drive for a few miles... This was the first time we had ever killed anything, and in one half-hour we ran over a large snake, a toad, and a tiny chicken.

The Baroness Campbell
Von Laurentz,
My Motor Milestones, 1913

Fig. 8

If one's own motor boy turns out to be equally slapdash then he should at least be trained to bag roadkill of a slightly more culinarily useful character than snakes and toads.

Reference should be made to Chapter Six in the hope of directing him to mow down better-quality game.

On balance, it might be better to dispense with staff altogether and emulate the routes taken by rakish motorists of the interwar years. In the 1920s it became tremendously chic for the rich to motor down to the French Riviera during the summer months. Prior to this the fashionable set had only wintered there, preferring to move to cooler climes in July and August, but American socialites Gerald and Sara Murphy popularised the coast by holding dazzling parties and inviting chums such as F. Scott Fitzgerald, Hemingway, Cocteau, Picasso and Dorothy Parker. Therefore, a gentleman enamoured of the heat and with a penchant for recreating the golden age of motoring should consider a summer run down to the Côte d'Azur, perhaps liaising with one's yacht, no doubt moored off Antibes, Nice, St-Tropez or Monte Carlo. Many splendid jaunts can be engaged upon as the scorching heat fades:

> *When six o'clock comes round you begin to stir, and you get out your car from her opulent garage nearby and you quietly begin to climb an olive growing hill and then another and then a third, and with the sun setting and the night air getting into your carburettor with most heady results, you drive on and on until perhaps at 2,000 or 3,000 feet up, you come to a rest on a little balcony of the Alps overlooking the sleeping Mediterranean. And there, amid the cool grey rocks and the tamaracks, with Corsica lying out on the horizon like a little dark cloud, you get out that very carefully chosen supper you brought from Monte Carlo.*

John Prioleau, *Motoring for Women*, 1925

RACES, RALLIES AND EVENTS

Returning to British shores in late summer, and possibly teetering on the edge of depression on his comedown from the heady excitements of the holiday season, the clubbable chap might hanker to give his vehicle an airing closer to home. For the motoring gent, if his steed is confined to its stable for any amount of time, he will undoubtedly contrive an excuse to put it through its paces:

There is a monster in the stable who has to be exercised, and from time to time you hear his brothers hooting to him as they rush past along the road, while the irresistible feeling grows on you that you must obey their cry, and start on your ride answering with Valkyrie-like cry the invitation that has been wafted on the sweet summer air.

Lady Jeune, quoted in Alexander Bell's
The Complete Motorist, 1904

Stirred by such symbolism and compelled by his innate urge to show off horribly, the gentleman motorist will not be slow to seek out new opportunities for causing the public to gape in wonderment at his chrome, his coachwork, his accelerating and swerving propensities and, in particular, his spectacular motoring outfits.

Thankfully such opportunities are never thin on the ground. Throughout the United Kingdom and Europe and throughout the year, like-minded individuals – enthusiasts, exhibitionists, peacocks and swaggerers – get together for vintage rallies, races and events. A gent is liable to get rather overexcited at the prospect of visiting such fixtures, but he should be aware that not everyone, and especially not his lady-love, is guaranteed to share his passion (**Fig. 9** overleaf).

Possibly the best place for the gentleman enthusiast to start is Brooklands, the world's first purpose-built motor-racing circuit, constructed at Weybridge, Surrey in 1907, where the Vintage Sports Car Club hold several events each year; or the Silverstone Classic; or the Classic Nostalgia Meeting at Shelsley Walsh where speed hill climbs have been held without a break (wartime excepted) since 1905. At the Goodwood Revival one can mix with the sort of people who realise that stylish motor cars and preposterously flamboyant clothing represent two sides of the same coin. Here a gent can really feel at home and get his teeth into nostalgia. He has the option of merely turning up, being seen, picnicking, spectating and dandying about a bit; or, if he is more robustly inclined, entering a few races and winning hands down in between rounds of canasta or cucumber sandwiches.

Another event that the devil-may-care fellow will of course positively itch to take part in is the Le Mans Classic, which was only instigated in 2002 but recreates all the thrill of taking part in the *24 Heures du Mans* endurance races pre-1979. Here one can register as a 'gentleman driver' (a non-professional enthusiast) and knock spots off the competition, who are likely to be a bit foreign and therefore well worth knocking spots off.

During the autumn the gent might tire of hurtling around at breakneck speed and opt for the potentially more sedate London to Brighton Veteran Car Run. This non-competitive event commemorates the Emancipation Run of 14 November 1896, which celebrated the relaxation of laws governing vehicles on the highway, increasing the speed limit to 14 miles per hour and dispensing with our fellow with the red flag (see Chapter Five). The main skill in this event is managing to keep one's vehicle moving. This is easier said than done, especially if one isn't mechanically gifted. It is essential to take along one passenger who

Fig. 9

knows what to do just in case you shudder to an unceremonious stop. A car such as the 1903 Panhard & Levassor is ideal for this. Dress up to the nines and you are likely to be showered in adulation *en route* by spectators and impressionable youths, who may well exhibit their enthusiasm in unusual ways:

> *Why do little boys always throw their hats into the road, so that Juggernaut-like a motor car may run over them? An experienced motor driver told me the other day that they were sometimes dangerous, as they got caught up by the machinery or in the wheels, giving some trouble to extricate them. He found this happened so often that whenever a boy threw his cap into the road he stopped, picked it up, and putting it in his pocket went on. He was soon so well known on the various roads in his part of the country that the little boys left him alone, but before they realised the means by which he stopped their pleasantry he became the owner of over eighty caps!*
>
> Lady Jeune, *Autocar* magazine, 1902

The grand larceny of schoolboy headgear cannot be recommended in this day and age. 'Youth' now tends to know its rights and confiscation of their personal property could result in one being brought in for a humiliating dressing-down at one's local police station.

TRANSPORTING CHILDREN

One element of getting away from it all that tends to put a bit of a dampener on the whole enterprise is the fact that if you have children, then you are usually expected to take them along with you.

When a young man first contemplates starting a family, he may be drawn to the idea, not only by the look of pleading insistence on his wife's face, but also by sentimental images of parenthood: the patter of tiny feet, the first fumbling attempts at articulating the word 'Da-Da', initiations into the pleasures of cricket and gin, and, of course, the fervent hope that they will be there to look after you when you have reached your dotage. One image that does not immediately spring to mind is that of sitting behind the wheel of a sensible family car undertaking the interminable car journeys that rearing offspring will inevitably entail; and a good thing too, for surely if a prospective father were ever to be burdened by such an insight into the future he would undoubtedly run screaming for the hills or at the very least the nearest vasectomy clinic.

The pairing of children with the motor car is one of the most disastrous combinations since Pandora picked up her newly acquired wooden casket one wet afternoon and thought to herself: 'Surely, one little peek can't do any harm.' When transported singularly and on short runs, children are just about manageable, but given a brood of two, three or four on a holiday run lasting several hours and it is almost impossible to imagine anything more straining to a gentleman's nerves and challenging to his sangfroid. The chief problem is that children are possessed with daemon-like reserves of energy. When set loose, they seem to enjoy nothing more than to endlessly run around in circles, screeching loudly, for no discernible reason. So confine the maverick beasts in a sealed metal box on wheels for hours on end and you are simply asking for trouble.

To start with, children have a very different concept of the passage of time from their adult counterparts. To them 60 minutes of inactivity is an unbearable chasm of misery which if not totally filled must be endlessly moaned about. Thus the incessant and familiar chorus of 'I'm bored' and 'Are we there yet?', or with older age groups the slightly more imaginative: 'How long is two and a half hours in seconds, Daddy?'; or perhaps: 'Papa, what exactly is time anyway?' By the time you get to question four, you know that something needs to be done and done sharpish. For older children, a simple bribe or blackmail tends to be quite effective, but for younger ones, who haven't quite got to grips with the art of emotional commerce, then discipline may be the only alternative. If a five-year-old is playing up, for example, then it is an acknowledged technique to get him to sit on the 'naughty step'. In the context of a motor car, the naughty step will

Fig. 10 The recommended travel arrangements for particularly unbiddable children.

happen to be any old doorstep you happen to be passing at the time. Plonking little Algernon down, tell him he mustn't move until he is told to. Then simply drive off, allowing him to contemplate the error of his ways, until you reappear ten minutes later, no doubt having calmed down a bit with the aid of a half of Shires at the hostelry on the other side of the village. Of course, this technique does mean he may require expensive corrective therapy in later life to help him get over his 'abandonment issues', but this may be outweighed by the short-term benefits. For particularly recalcitrant children, the travel arrangements as seen in **Fig. 10** are recommended.

Apart from disciplinary issues, children will spend a good proportion of any journey either *feeling* ill or actively *being* ill. Other than the infernal moaning it produces, the *feeling* ill part isn't much of a problem, it is only when it wells up and overflows into actually

Fig. 11

being ill that a gent needs to worry. 'Seeping' ailments such as travel sickness, the norovirus or dysentery are guaranteed to strike when you are stuck on a motorway with a further 20 miles to go before the nearest exit. At times like these you will actually feel rather relieved that you had to sacrifice your delightful 1955 Jaguar XK 140 for a utilitarian 'family' car, as the damage all those bodily fluids could have done to the beautiful beige leather interior might easily have pushed you over the edge.

With buying a family car in mind, despite the rank humiliation of having to contemplate such a thing, we should now give some thought to its selection. As with any other vehicle you purchase, it is bound to reflect your attitude towards life, and just because you have brought forth progeny, this is no reason to abandon any concept of style. If they were still readily available on the market, the gentleman would no doubt select a Dymaxion or the Burney Streamline (see Chapter Two), as they both combine style with ample space for a growing brood. However, a gentleman of limited means (but with a soul firmly in Elysium) should opt for a suitable vintage model, perhaps the 1928 Model A Ford Roadster illustrated

Fig. 12

in **Fig. 11**. As you can see, the open-top design is perfectly suited to softening the effects of any inane babble or complaints that may arise from the rear seat. The rear seat itself is a 'dicky', which essentially means that your little cherubs are being transported in the boot, which should be regarded as 'character building' – especially when undertaking journeys on days of torrential rain or blizzard.

There is a wrong-headed minority on the roads today (admittedly living in places such as Fulham or Alderley Edge) who coddle their infants by carrying them about in unsavoury-looking four-by-fours. The outward sign of such over-protectiveness is a vehicle so burdened with bull bars, roll bars and chunky bumpers that it begins to resemble a Humvee on active service in Afghanistan (**Fig. 12**). Such a vehicle is not only displeasing to the eye, but also insufferably vulgar, and if there is one thing that the gentleman motorist regards as unforgivable, that thing is vulgarity.

CAR WINDOW SURFING

The harassed gentleman motorist will find that the key to making long journeys with relatives and offspring pass more pleasantly is to do one's best to keep them adequately entertained. Older relatives can be fobbed off with newspapers, books and packets of bonbons, whilst children can be kept occupied by long rounds of I Spy or Dumb Crambo, singalongs, card games, squabbling with their siblings or quietly stupefying themselves on Nintendo consoles.

A new addition to this list of in-car entertainment is the increasingly popular hobby of 'car window surfing'. Based on the natural zeal that pet dogs and children exhibit for poking their heads out of the windows and sunroof whilst travelling at high speeds, window surfing seeks to harness the invigorating effects of air stream and velocity as an entertainment for all the family.

A refreshingly dangerous sport, in an age of Health and Safety gone mad, it is recommended that you restrict your window surfing activities to featureless landscapes, preferably free from trees, hedges, road signs, members of the constabulary, livestock, other traffic and civilisation in general, and to these ends, the famous Bonneville Salt Flats of Utah or, alternatively, Norfolk might suggest themselves as suitable options. You should also make sure to take out adequate third-party and personal insurance to cover damage to pets, children, paintwork and various exposed extremities, such as your head. With these few rudimentary precautions in place, hours of devil-may-care pleasure await you.

The novitiate will probably approach this new sport with some caution at first and may wish to conduct an experiment or two, observing the simple antics of his pet canine (**Fig. 13a**), but before he knows it he will be joining in the fun, shoving his own head out of the window and howling *The Rime of the Ancient Mariner* at full belt into the wind as he hurtles along the M6.

Figs. 13b to 13g illustrate just a few of the many and varied possibilities that window surfing has to offer:

Fig. 13a Although a gentleman would usually favour a majestic breed of dog such as a Pharaoh Hound or Airedale Terrier, it is remarkable how one's ladyfriend's embarrassing pooch can be streamlined to perfection by a brisk headwind.

Fig. 13b All manner of gentlemanly pursuits can be adapted to the requirements of window surfing. Here, a fellow keeps his peregrine falcon in trim by requiring it to trail his Wolseley during his frequent dashes to his local turf accountant.

Fig. 13c Ladies are genetically programmed to fall for totally unsuitable, louche young gentlemen who drive open-topped sports cars at breakneck speed. What could be better than combining the allure of your MG with a window surfing re-enactment of a particularly soppy scene from one of her very favourite soppy Hollywood blockbusters?

Fig. 13d The latest trend of the blandly aspirational is to send their infants to so-called 'baby gyms'. This ensures that they grow up every bit as unimaginative as their parents. This little fellow is being given a better start in life, from day one, living in the fast lane.

Fig. 13e This fellow might be thought to have taken leave of his senses by taking his favourite filly out for a spin, but there is method in his madness. With 200 smackers riding on this particular three-legged nag in the 4.20 at Cheltenham, he has had to resort to slightly desperate measures to ensure that it crosses the line ahead of the competition.

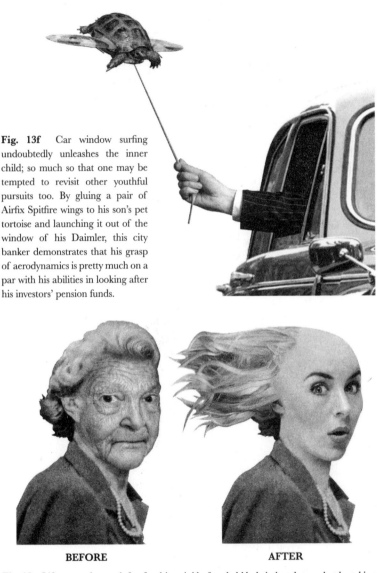

Fig. 13f Car window surfing undoubtedly unleashes the inner child; so much so that one may be tempted to revisit other youthful pursuits too. By gluing a pair of Airfix Spitfire wings to his son's pet tortoise and launching it out of the window of his Daimler, this city banker demonstrates that his grasp of aerodynamics is pretty much on a par with his abilities in looking after his investors' pension funds.

BEFORE

AFTER

Fig. 13g Life cannot be much fun for this wrinkle-faced old lady in her dotage, but by taking her for a literally hair-raising high-speed drive in the back of his convertible, her caring nephew has allowed her to fleetingly regain the radiance of her lost complexion by using the phenomenon of 'drag' as an impromptu face-lifting device.

IN SUMMARY:

Ten Rules for the Gentleman Motorist

1. A gentleman motorist recognises only two speeds – a moderate tootle and a fair old lick.

2. The gentleman motorist eschews mundane traffic manoeuvres, and instead errs on the side of the impressively flamboyant.

3. The selection of a vehicle should be based on the shininess of its metalwork, the voluptuousness of its design and its pre-1973 vintage.

4. Never venture behind the wheel of a car unless in suitable attire accompanied with goggles and a pipe. It is impossible for a gentleman motorist to wear too much tweed.

5. Always greet members of the constabulary with a distant respect and avoid endearments such as 'My dear' or 'Me old china'.

6. Never take the names of Stirling Moss, Alfred Dunhill, W.O. Bentley or Alec Issigonis in vain.

7. A gentleman regards the laws of the highway merely as a starting point on which to build his own artistic theories and extemporisations.

8. Treat fellow road users with the utmost courtesy even if most of them are hapless fools. A gentleman's motto is 'I doff therefore I am'.

9. A gentleman must make a study of car mechanics, but only to the point where he is able to convincingly fake expertise beneath the bonnet.

10. Remember the days of the London to Brighton Veteran Car Run, Silverstone Classic and Goodwood Revival and keep them holy.

BIBLIOGRAPHY

Colonel Harold Atherton, *Simplified Motoring. The beginner's complete guide to car driving and the test, etc* (Simpkin Marshall, London, 1938)

Michael Austen, *Learning to Drive a Car* (Odhams Press, London, 1961)

The Autocar magazine, April–June 1902

The Autocar magazine, *Useful Hints and Tips for Automobilists* (Iliffe & Sons, London, 1906)

Charles L. Baudry de Saunier, *The Art of Motor Driving* (Iliffe & Sons, London, 1909)

Algernon E. Berriman, *Motoring: An introduction to the car and the art of driving it. With forty-eight plates and many diagrams* (Methuen & Co., London, 1914)

British School of Motoring, *How to Drive a Car* (Temple Press Limited, London,1950)

C.W. Brown, *The ABC of Motoring* (H.J. Drane, London, 1909)

K.R.G. Browne and W. Heath Robinson, *How to Be a Motorist* (Hutchinson & Co., London, 1939)

The Baroness Campbell Von Laurentz, *My Motor Milestones* (Herbert Jenkins, London, 1913)

Gilbert A. Christian, *Safety First for School and Home* (Hodder & Stoughton, London, 1925)

Richard Alexander Douglas, *Common Sense in Driving Your Car* (Longmans, Green & Co., New York, 1936)

'A Four-Inch Driver', *The Chauffeur's Companion* (Mills & Boon, London, 1909)

John Harrison, *The Boy's Book of the Motor-Car* (Humphrey Milford, London, 1926)

Leonard Henslowe, *Buying a Car?* (Hutchinson & Co., London, 1928)

Felix Johnson, *How to Pass the Driving Test* (Anthony Gibbs & Phillips, London, 1964)

John Henry Knight, *A Catechism of the Motor Car* (Crosby Lockwood & Son, London, 1908)

F. Llewellyn-Jones, *The Road Traffic Act 1930* (Sweet & Maxwell, London, 1931)

The staff of 'The Light Car and Cyclecar', *How to Drive a Light Car or a Cyclecar* (Temple Press, London, 1917)

Professor Archibald M. Low, *The Wonder Book of Inventions* (Ward, Lock & Co., London & Melbourne, 1930)

The staff of *The Motor, How to Drive a Motorcar: A key to the subtleties of motoring* (Temple Press, London, 1914)

Lawrence Nathan, *Car Driving in Two Weeks* (Elliot Right Way Books, Kingswood, Surrey 1963)

Raymond Needham, *Love in a Motor-Car* (Andrew Melrose, London, 1912)

Leonard Pringle, *Driving Lessons in Eight Easy Stages* (Oliver & Boyd, Edinburgh & London, 1955)

John Prioleau, *Motoring for Women* (Geoffrey Bles, London, 1925)

L.V.E. Smith, *How to Drive a Car Correctly* (Crosby Lockwood & Son, London, 1926)

Humfrey Ewan Symons, *How to Pass the Driving Test* (L. Dickson & Thompson, London, 1935)

R.M.T. Treeve, *Real Road Safety* (Acme Printing Co., Portsmouth, 1946)

Richard Twelvetrees, *All About Motoring* (Hodder & Stoughton, London, 1924)

A.B. Filson Young, *The Complete Motorist* (Methuen & Co., London, 1904)

ACKNOWLEDGEMENTS

Many thanks to Dougal Cawley, who has provided continual advice, support and photographs whilst thankfully expecting no fee and therefore getting none. His only request is that I mention his estimable tyre company, Longstone Classic Tyres, contactable for all your vintage tyre requirements via **www.longstonetyres.co.uk**

Equal thanks go to Canadian horologist, Rob Trueman, who also provided advice and photographs – chiefly of various weird and wonderful vehicles, only the merest fraction of which have made it into this volume.

Further assistance and support was furnished by Maria Teresa Gavazzi (psychological wellbeing tzar), Nigel Burch (ukulele maestro of this parish) for consenting to be *Honest John* on page 40, Susan Smith (agent and friend), Torquil Arbuthnot (car enthusiast and louche man-about-town), Amanda Hill for her honest opinions and encouragement, Duncan Pickstock for some helpful discussions over a pint or two, Helen Brocklehurst (strangely trusting editor), James Tims (the man we can thank for getting permission to reproduce Dunhill's Bobby Finders poster), Donna Wood for primping my text and Tracey Butler for adding professional polish to my layout.

Many thanks to curator Zia Fernandez-Ibarreche for permission to use images on pages 53, 56, 57 (Windshield pipe), 60, 61 and 64, courtesy of the Alfred Dunhill Museum and Archive. Thanks to Tom Oates for the photograph of the Jowett Jupiter Convertible, page 47, and James Royle for the photograph of the 1954 Bentley Continental R-type, page 176. Thanks also to Getty Images for source images on page 128 (Bert Hardy/Picture Post/Hulton Archive/Getty Images), and page 130 (Keystone/Hulton Archive/Getty Images).